I FLOURISH

Your Guide to Proactive Mental Health

JUDD ALLEN, Ph.D.

Human Resources Institute, LLC
www.healthyculture.com
151 Dunder Road
Burlington, Vermont 05401 USA
JuddA@healthyculture.com
(802) 862-8855

Ordering Information
Quantity sales. Special discounts are available on quantity purchases by organizations, associations, and others. For details, contact the publisher.
Library of Congress Cataloging-in-Publication Data
Names: Allen, Judd, 1958-author.
I Flourish: Your Guide to Proactive Mental Health
Description: Burlington, Vermont: HealthyCulture.com [2024] | Includes bibliographical references.
Identifiers: eBook ISBN 978-0-941703-52-9; paperback ISBN 978-0-941703-50-5 Hardcover/Cloth ISBN 978-0-941703-51-2
Subjects: NONFICTION/Self-Help/Mental Health

Cover photograph of Judd Allen by Karen Pike of www.kpikephoto.com.

Contents

Acknowledgments

This book ambitiously addresses 27 unique proactive mental health attitudes and behaviors. My primary role has been identifying the attitudes and behaviors supporting mental well-being and accumulating information about them. My goals were to provide a wide variety of choices to those seeking to improve their mental well-being and develop actionable information. I took full advantage of large language models (LLMs) to better understand what is known about these attitudes and behaviors. I am grateful to all those whose ideas and research findings have been incorporated into the LLMs. This new technology left me feeling more like an editor than an author. I have found research for this book to be very informative and enjoyable. Please read the books recommended at the end of each chapter. Their authors are among the subject matter experts. I hope this book will start a conversation about adopting lifestyle practices that support our mental well-being.

    Emma Friedman helped build recommended reading lists. She also assisted in conducting and analyzing the

Proactive Mental Health Self-Assessment. We thank the volunteers for completing the self-assessment. Their collective experiences enhanced our understanding of proactive mental health goals.

Thanks to Don Ardell, Michael Arloski, David Ballard, Craig Becker, Jim Carman, Howard Goldberg, Bill Hettler, Joe Leutzinger, Tad Mitchell, Michael O'Donnell, Erin Pataky, Gillian Pieper, Kay Ryan, Samia Simurro, Marie-Josee Shaar, Ewa Stelmasiak, Elaine Sullivan, and Jack Travis. These leaders share a vision that includes both kindness and flourishing.

My close friends and family generously provided their feedback and encouragement. Mollie Allen, Richard Blount, Andrea Melville, Jonathan Sands, Mary Sochet, and Clay Warren were a big help.

Statement about Kinder and More Inclusive Language

This book is about mental health and emotional well-being. There has been a long history of discrimination and stigmatization associated with this topic. One way to help rectify this has been to avoid terms like mental illness and use substitute language such as mental health condition, mental wellness challenges, and neurodiverse/neurodivergent conditions. I am using the term mental health challenges to address mental health discrimination and *stigmatization.*

We now know humans are extraordinarily diverse in sexual identity and sexual orientation. The English language needs to honor that diversity. So, where you may have seen *he/she*, I'm going to use *they* or *them.*

Chapter 1

To Flourish

To flourish
1: to grow luxuriantly: THRIVE
2a: to achieve success: PROSPER
b: to be in a state of activity or production
c: to reach a height of development or influence
"FLOURISH." MERRIAM-WEBSTER.COM DICTIONARY

THE TERM "FLOURISH" is often used in various disciplines to describe a state of optimal functioning and well-being. To flourish is not merely to be free from mental health challenges or adversity; it involves positive engagement with life, realizing one's potential, and having a sense of meaning and purpose.

Flourishing stands in contrast to languishing. When languishing, a person is neither mentally challenged nor flourishing but instead exists in emotional and psychological limbo. Too many of us live one day, week, month, or year away from the precipice of mental health challenges. This is suboptimal and leaves us vulnerable. My goal with this book is to help us move away from the precipice of mental health challenges and instead move towards flourishing.

Nearly 50 percent of us will experience mental health challenges during our lifetimes. At last count, 21 percent of U.S. adults—52.9 million—experience mental health challenges annually. Globally, 12 billion working days are lost every year due to poor mental health. There is an epidemic of mental health challenges among young people. Mental health challenges among parents are having a devastating effect on children and families. Mental health resources are insufficient to meet the needs of those struggling. Developing such resources requires time and lots of money. Prevention is the only scalable and affordable remedy for the current mental health crisis.

Fortunately, we can adopt proactive mental health attitudes and behaviors that reduce the chances of being afflicted with anxiety, depression, substance abuse, and other mental health challenges. Importantly, these proactive mental health attitudes and behaviors result in happier, healthier, and more productive lives.

In the 1970s, a similar challenge and opportunity spawned the wellness movement. This movement addressed premature death, cancer, and heart disease. We recognized that lifestyle practices could be important for lowering disease risk and improving overall quality of life. This book builds on the original wellness vision by focusing on how our attitudes and behaviors can support mental health and well-being.

You probably know through life experiences that many attitudes and behaviors are good for your mental health. I, for one, have long been aware that running clears my head and improves my mood. Physical activity has been important for my mental health. This awareness and my connection to the wellness movement raised my awareness of other ways to strengthen our resilience and well-being. I have been thrilled to discover that there are many things we can do to improve our mental well-being.

In this book, I discuss 27 proactive mental health behaviors and attitudes that enhance mental health and protect against mental health challenges. Each strategy represents an opportunity to avoid mental health challenges and to achieve optimal well-being. You can choose from many flourishing strategies. There is no single thing that everyone must do to be healthier; each of us can choose what is most meaningful and accessible to us.

As this field evolves, additional proactive mental health behaviors and attitudes will be discovered. I have organized the 27 proactive mental health attitudes and behaviors into broad categories or building blocks, such as social connection, purpose, safety, presence, and adaptability. The chapters in this book explore the full range of proactive mental health attitudes and behaviors. Chapter 2 features self-assessments to help you prioritize your proactive mental health goals. You'll assess your current practices and plan to address those factors undermining your well-being. Chapter 2 also discusses a step-by-step approach to change. Chapters

3 through 29 explore what is known about each strategy. As you build your knowledge and skill sets, you will take flourishing to the next level. You'll learn about the most common myths and misunderstandings about each topic. You'll learn how to track your success. The chapters also include lists of recommended books to further your learning.

I Flourish explains how, with the support of others, we can better secure personal mental well-being. This is my third book on proactive mental health. *We Flourish*, a management guidebook about creating supportive work cultures, introduced the proactive mental health approach. *Better Together* guides family, friends, and coworkers in their efforts to provide effective peer support to each other.

Reader Tip: This book is very comprehensive. Make your reading more manageable by using the self-assessment in Chapter 2 to identify the chapters that are most relevant to you now.

Setting Proactive Mental Health Goals

"A goal without a plan is just a wish."
- Antoine de Saint-Exupéry

"The good life is a process, not a state of being. It is a direction, not a destination."
- Carl Rogers

Proactive mental health is about preventing mental health challenges and achieving optimal well-being. When picking goals and strategies, it is often helpful to have many choices. If one strategy is unpleasant, you can try additional strategies. We can substitute or mix in additional activities if we tire of our routine. If there are obstacles to maintaining a particular practice, you can pick a strategy with fewer barriers.

Proactive mental health is an overlapping matrix of 27 behaviors and attitudes organized into six building blocks.

Building Blocks of Proactive Mental Health

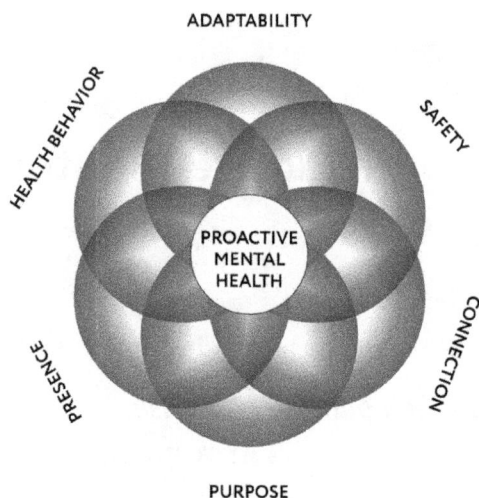

You already have proactive mental health strengths. You are also likely to have at least one attitude or behavior that could be improved. In a survey of wellness professionals, most respondents (73%) had attempted to improve their proactive mental health attitudes in the past year. Roughly half of the survey respondents (52%) reported that they had helped another person with their mental health. In other words, you're in good company: your friends, family, and coworkers are probably working to address their mental health, too.

The following Proactive Mental Health Self-Assessment provides a way to see how you are doing. It examines the full scope of attitudes and behaviors that promote emotional well-being. You can use the results from this self-assessment to help you set proactive mental health goals.

Proactive Mental Health Self-Assessment

Proactive mental health is a constellation of behaviors and attitudes that prevent mental health challenges and increase overall mental well-being. The following self-assessment asks about 27 current practices. Your answers will help prioritize efforts to support mental health.

Instructions: *Using the five-point scale, rate how often you experience each proactive mental health attitude or behavior.*

5 Always
4 Often
3 Sometimes
2 Rarely
1 Never
NA Not applicable

ATTITUDES AND BEHAVIOR	Current Practice
Presence	
Are you able to focus on the here and now?	5 4 3 2 1 NA
Do you declutter your life so you can experience inner peace?	5 4 3 2 1 NA
Do you practice daily stress management techniques like walking, meditation, or yoga?	5 4 3 2 1 NA

Connection	
Are you able to love and be loved?	5 4 3 2 1 NA
Do you spend time with friends most days?	5 4 3 2 1 NA
Can you forgive?	5 4 3 2 1 NA
Are you grateful?	5 4 3 2 1 NA
Can you trust others, and are you trustworthy?	5 4 3 2 1 NA
Are you good at teamwork?	5 4 3 2 1 NA
Are you kind?	5 4 3 2 1 NA
Adaptability	
Can you handle disappointment?	5 4 3 2 1 NA
Do you persist in the face of challenges?	5 4 3 2 1 NA
Are you open to trying new ways of doing things?	5 4 3 2 1 NA
Do you consider your strengths before taking on tasks and challenges?	5 4 3 2 1 NA
Do you avoid seeing problems or bad news as permanent, pervasive (affecting all things), or personal (about you)?	5 4 3 2 1 NA
Purpose	
Do you feel like you are making a difference?	5 4 3 2 1 NA
Do you regularly do things that give your life meaning?	5 4 3 2 1 NA
Do you experience passion and commitment?	5 4 3 2 1 NA

Safety	
Do you feel financially secure?	5 4 3 2 1 NA
Are you free from physical and emotional violence and abuse?	5 4 3 2 1 NA
Do you live, work, and play in healthy physical environments?	5 4 3 2 1 NA
Health Behavior	
Are you current on your preventive medical health screenings?	5 4 3 2 1 NA
Do you get help with mental health problems early on?	5 4 3 2 1 NA
Do you eat a healthy diet?	5 4 3 2 1 NA
Do you drink alcohol or use other recreational drugs moderately, if at all?	5 4 3 2 1 NA
Do you get adequate rest?	5 4 3 2 1 NA
Do you take part in 30 minutes or more of physical activity most days of the week?	5 4 3 2 1 NA

Review your responses. How are you doing with proactive mental health? A person can be mentally healthy without achieving all 27 practices. Here are recommendations for getting the most out of your responses to this self-assessment:

- **Review your strengths.** Strengths are those questions with scores of four or five. Acknowledging the aspects of proactive mental health already in place is an excellent place to start. Explore those positive qualities. How can you use them to address any remaining opportunities for improvement? Explore how you developed these lifestyle strengths. See if there's something to learn from your past successes. Build upon these strengths when approaching areas that still need attention. Proactive mental health strengths are important because they indicate past success and are the building blocks for future progress.

- **Review those areas that need attention.** Areas that need attention are the questions with scores of one, two, or three. Focus on the areas where you have both a need and desire to change. You don't have to address all low-scoring areas, especially all at once; it's okay to be satisfied with how things stand.

- **Examine any goals not covered in the assessment.** Reflect on what has been important to your mental health. Did the self-assessment miss something important? Hopefully, the questions broadened your perspective on how you can address your mental health. Determine whether your needs were adequately addressed and any gaps or variations that reflect your interests better.

- **Explore possible connections between goals.** Proactive mental health goals often address overlapping behaviors, so one goal can spill over into other purposes. Proactive mental health is an integrative process that engages the mind, body, and spirit. By examining possible links among goals, you may develop new practices that address many goals simultaneously. For example, a daily yoga practice could help you address physical activity and presence goals. Similarly, someone seeking to lower stress may find sleep, exercise, nutrition, and increased social engagement helpful. Consider prioritizing changes that accomplish multiple goals.

- **Examine personal passion, motivation, and enthusiasm for the goals.** Your chosen goals must be important enough to inspire your ongoing commitment. Enthusiasm and drive make changes easier to maintain and more enjoyable. Consider multiple purposes for achieving your goals. What are all the benefits you might enjoy by achieving your goals? For example, in addition to self-preservation, some people pursue proactive mental health to be better role models for their children or grandchildren.

- **Decide on the amount of change you can commit to.** Everyone has limits, and our limits can change with our circumstances. A change must be important enough to maintain your interest and engagement. Goals must be big enough to be challenging but not so big that they feel overwhelming.

A Step-by-Step Approach to Lasting Change

If you are like most people, you can identify one or more opportunities to enhance your proactive mental health. You can set yourself up for long-term success by adopting a step-by-step approach that addresses the barriers to lasting change.

Step One: Separate Facts from Fiction

There are many misunderstandings about proactive mental health. For example, believing you must be a yogi or guru to be fully present is an all-too-common myth. We can integrate mindfulness into everyday activities, such as engaging in physical activity or relaxing with a cup of coffee. You don't need to be an expert in any area you want to change, but it's a good idea to clear away common misunderstandings. We address such myths and misunderstandings throughout this book; more are debunked in the recommended books.

You can skip to the chapters that address your primary change goals using the following table. These chapters were written to provide a firm overview of the important facts related to each behavior or attitude identified in the Proactive Mental Health Self-Assessment.

PROACTIVE MENTAL HEALTH SELF-ASSESSMENT QUESTIONS	RELATED BOOK CHAPTER AND PAGE NUMBER
Presence	
Are you able to focus on the here and now?	Chapter 3, Page 21
Do you declutter your life so you can experience inner peace?	Chapter 4, Page 29
Do you practice daily stress management techniques like walking, meditation, or yoga?	Chapter 5, Page 37
Connection	
Are you able to love and be loved?	Chapter 6, Page 49

Do you spend time with friends most days?	Chapter 7, Page 59
Can you forgive?	Chapter 8, Page 69
Are you grateful?	Chapter 9, Page 77
Can you trust others, and are you trustworthy?	Chapter 10, Page 85
Are you good at teamwork?	Chapter 11, Page 95
Are you kind?	Chapter 12, Page 105
Adaptability	
Can you handle disappointment?	Chapter 13, Page119
Do you persist in the face of challenges?	Chapter 14, Page 129
Are you open to trying new ways of doing things?	Chapter 15, Page 139
Do you consider your strengths before taking on tasks and challenges?	Chapter 16, Page 149
Do you avoid seeing problems or bad news as permanent, pervasive (affecting all things), or personal (about you)?	Chapter 17, Page 159
Purpose	
Do you feel like you are making a difference?	Chapter 18, Page 173
Do you regularly do things that give your life meaning?	Chapter 19, Page 183
Do you experience passion and commitment?	Chapter 20, Page 195

Safety	
Do you feel financially secure?	Chapter 21, Page 211
Are you free from physical and emotional violence and abuse?	Chapter 22, Page 223
Do you live, work, and play in healthy physical environments?	Chapter 23, Page 233
Health Behavior	
Are you current on your preventive medical health screenings?	Chapter 24, Page 251
Do you get help with mental health problems early on?	Chapter 25, Page 261
Do you eat a healthy diet?	Chapter 26, Page 271
Do you drink alcohol or use other recreational drugs moderately, if at all?	Chapter 27, Page 283
Do you get adequate rest?	Chapter 28, Page 295
Do you take part in 30 minutes or more of physical activity most days of the week?	Chapter 29, Page 301

Step Two: Find or Build Yourself a Supportive Environment

Achieving and maintaining your goals is easier when you spend time in environments that support desired behaviors and attitudes. Consider how you can seek out or create those physical and cultural environments. This can be as simple as letting your coworkers, friends, and family know about your goals and how they might help you be successful. You may also find some new supportive groups or places. Classmates in a seminar on financial planning would, for example, be likely to support your efforts to achieve economic security. Volunteers at the local Humane Society will likely enthusiastically support your efforts to strengthen your sense of purpose by caring for animals.

Step Three: Make a Plan

Lifestyle change is an ongoing process that begins with deciding to make a change, choosing how to proceed, and planning how you will track and celebrate your progress. The books recommended in each chapter share best practices and case stories that can be templates for making your plan.

Step Four: Keep Track and Tune In

The early days of any change are exciting. You are tackling an important personal goal. The reasons are fresh in your mind, and you are paying attention. This action phase is important, and so is maintenance. The maintenance phase is when supportive environments and routines keep you on track. As your initial excitement and focus decline, maintain your momentum by keeping track of your progress and leaning on your supportive environments.

Step Five: Reach Out to Others

Helping others accomplish similar goals can help you be successful, too. Explaining your efforts reaffirms your public commitment and provides an opportunity to review your plan. If your peers are successful, they will become a part of your supportive subculture. Helping others also supports a sense of self-worth and well-being.

Goal-Setting Checklist

Before turning to the next chapter, summarize your goal-setting decisions. The following checklist will help you determine whether you have covered key ideas.

- ☐ I identified existing lifestyle strengths and considered how I could develop and maintain them.
- ☐ I identified opportunities for improvement.
- ☐ I determined which proactive goals might be most important to me. I examined the benefits that matter most to me.
- ☐ I determined which personal change goals might be connected by common practices.
- ☐ I considered how much energy I can commit to pursuing my goals.
- ☐ I am ready to build a step-by-step plan to achieve lasting lifestyle change.

Proactive Mental Health Building Block: Presence

Being present, often referred to as mindfulness or living in the present moment, involves cultivating awareness of the present moment without judgment or attachment to past or future events. The following three chapters on living in the here and now, decluttering, and practicing stress management discuss increasing your ability to be present. You are probably already engaged in some of these strategies. Reading the following three chapters will likely reveal additional opportunities for improvement.

Being present is a valuable proactive mental health strategy. Here are some ways being present can impact mental well-being:

- **Reduced stress and anxiety:** Mindfulness practices help you detach from worries about the future or regrets about the past, reducing stress and anxiety levels. You can let go of racing thoughts and experience greater calm by focusing on the present moment.

- **Improved emotional regulation:** Being present makes you more aware of your emotions as they arise. This increased awareness helps recognize and understand feelings without getting overwhelmed. With practice, mindfulness can lead to improved emotional regulation and the ability to respond to emotions in a healthier and more balanced manner.

- **Enhanced overall well-being:** When fully present, you can engage more fully in your daily activities and relationships. This leads to greater fulfillment, satisfaction, and enjoyment in life. Being present allows you to savor positive experiences, appreciate the little things, and develop a deeper connection with yourself and others.

- **Reduced rumination:** Rumination is common in many mental health conditions, such as depression and anxiety. It involves repetitive, negative thinking patterns focused on past events or future worries. Being present helps break the cycle of rumination by redirecting attention to the present moment and promoting a more positive and constructive mindset.

- **Increased self-compassion:** Mindfulness allows you to observe your thoughts and emotions with non-judgmental acceptance. This practice fosters self-compassion, which involves treating yourself with kindness and understanding rather than being self-critical.

Understand How Culture Supports or Undermines Presence

Work, home, and community cultures shape your capacity to be present. If you live with others, take stock of how your housemates or family experience the present moment. Take stock of your friends, neighbors, and immediate coworkers, too. Are they living in the moment, paying attention to right now, or are they distracted and looking forward or backward?

Different cultures have varying perspectives on time. Some cultures emphasize the importance of living in the present moment and savoring it, while others prioritize the past or future. For example, present-oriented cultures may value spontaneity, immediate gratification, and enjoying the present moment. In contrast, cultures with a future-oriented perspective may emphasize planning, delayed gratification, and striving for long-term goals.

The prevalent use of technology can significantly impact your ability to live in the present moment. Widespread technology adoption and constant connectivity may make it difficult to be fully present. Our phones and other devices provide distractions that demand our attention. The influence of digital devices and social media can fragment your focus and divert your attention from your immediate surroundings.

Your cultural environments influence your behavior and attitudes. Culture helps determine your role models and what is rewarded and recognized. Although you may choose to live differently, the easier path will be to adopt the behaviors of those around you in order to fit in. If you have a goal around cultivating presence, you'll be most successful if you spend time in environments where such presence is accepted and encouraged.

Chapter 3

Focus on the Here and Now

"The present moment is the only moment available to us, and it is the door to all moments."

- Thich Nhat Hanh

"The secret of health for both mind and body is not to mourn for the past, nor to worry about the future, but to live the present moment wisely and earnestly."

- Buddha

Focusing on the here and now refers to directing your attention and awareness to the present moment rather than dwelling on the past or worrying about the future. It involves fully engaging with your current experiences, thoughts, feelings, and sensations. Focusing on the here and now is a fundamental aspect of mindfulness, defined as purposefully paying attention to the present moment without judgment. It involves observing your thoughts and emotions without getting caught up in them as they arise.

The Benefits of Focusing on the Here and Now

Focusing on the present has numerous benefits, such as:

- **Reduced Stress and Anxiety**: When you can focus on the present moment, you can alleviate worries about the past or future. By directing your attention to the task at hand, you reduce overwhelm and promote a sense of calmness, which can help manage stress and anxiety.

- **Deepened Relationships and Communication**: Being present and focused during interactions with others strengthens your listening skills, empathy, and understanding. It fosters meaningful connections and effective communication by demonstrating respect and active engagement.

- **Increased Life Satisfaction**: Focus can contribute to your overall well-being. It promotes a sense of accomplishment, self-efficacy, and satisfaction in achieving goals. Additionally, being able to direct your attention and filter out distractions can lead to a greater sense of control, mindfulness, and inner peace.

- **Enhanced Productivity**: You become more productive when concentrating on a specific task or goal. The ability to focus allows you to work efficiently, complete tasks in a timely manner, and achieve your objectives.

- **Improved Performance:** Focused attention enhances performance in various domains, including work, academics, sports, and creative pursuits. By directing your mental resources toward the task at hand, you can optimize your skills, problem-solving abilities, and decision-making processes, leading to improved outcomes.

- **Heightened Learning and Information Processing:** Focus is critical in learning and information processing. When you concentrate on the material being presented or studied, you can better absorb, understand, and retain it. Focus facilitates deeper comprehension and enhances memory consolidation.

- **Increased Attention to Detail:** Focus allows you to pay attention to details and nuances that may otherwise go unnoticed. This heightened attention to detail can benefit tasks requiring precision, critical thinking, analysis, and error detection.

- **Enhanced Problem Solving:** Focus enables you to delve into complex problems, break them into manageable components, and explore potential solutions. It helps you maintain a clear train of thought, identify relevant information, and generate creative ideas to overcome challenges.

- **Heightened Creativity:** While focus is often associated with concentration, it also can facilitate divergent thinking and creativity. Immersing yourself in a task or idea allows you to explore different perspectives, make novel connections, and generate innovative solutions.

- **Improved Decision Making:** Focus allows you to gather and process relevant information, consider different options, and make informed decisions. It helps you filter out distractions, evaluate alternatives more objectively, and weigh the potential consequences of your choices.

Common Myths and Misunderstandings about Focusing on the Here and Now

How many of the following myths and misunderstandings are you familiar with?

Myth: "Focusing on the present means ignoring the past and future."

Reality: Focusing on the present moment involves cultivating mindfulness and awareness, which can enhance our ability to respond effectively to both past and future situations. Acknowledging and learning from past experiences while planning is essential for personal growth and well-being.

Myth: "Focusing on the here and now is a form of escapism."

Reality: Mindfulness emphasizes present-moment awareness and encourages individuals to acknowledge and accept their unpleasant or distressing experiences. By developing a non-judgmental attitude, mindfulness can help us process emotions and face challenges more effectively rather than escaping from them.

Myth: "Focusing on the here and now is incompatible with planning and goal setting."

Reality: Being fully present can enhance our capacity for effective planning and goal setting. By cultivating mindfulness, we develop a greater sense of clarity, focus, and intention, which can positively influence our ability to make decisions and take actions that align with our long-term aspirations.

Myth: "Focusing on the here and now is a cure-all for mental health issues."

Reality: While mindfulness has been shown to have numerous benefits for mental health, it is important to recognize that it is not a panacea or a standalone treatment for all mental health conditions, nor will mindfulness "fix" all of our challenges.

Self-Assessment: Focusing on the Here and Now

Ask yourself the following questions:

1. Can I stay engaged and attentive during tasks that require concentration?
2. How easily do I get distracted by external stimuli (such as noise, movement, or interruptions)?
3. Do I find it challenging to focus on one task for an extended period?
4. Can I resist the temptation to check my phone or engage in unrelated activities while working on a task?
5. Can I switch my attention between tasks or activities without difficulty?

6. Do I struggle to complete tasks or projects within a reasonable timeframe?
7. How well do I manage competing demands for my attention and prioritize tasks effectively?
8. Do I feel mentally fatigued or refreshed after engaging in tasks requiring sustained focus?
9. Am I aware of my attentional patterns and tendencies, such as when my focus starts to decline or when I'm more prone to distraction?

Each of these questions helps determine whether you are experiencing difficulties with being present. Most people can identify opportunities for improvement. Periodically check your experience. There are likely times when you will need to adjust your approach.

Improving Your Ability to Focus on the Here and Now

Fortunately, focusing on the here and now is a trainable skill. There are many mindfulness interventions, such as Mindfulness-Based Stress Reduction (MBSR) and Mindfulness-Based Cognitive Therapy (MBCT), which have been effective in treating various mental health challenges.

Focusing on the present is not limited to formal mindfulness practices. It can be integrated into daily life by paying attention to the present moment during routine activities like eating, walking, or engaging in hobbies.

Books about Being Present

The following books can help you learn to cultivate mindfulness and focus on the present moment.

The Art of Living: Peace and Freedom in the Here and Now. Thich Nhat Hanh's book offers practical guidance on living mindfully, embracing the present moment, and finding peace and happiness in everyday life.

Wherever You Go, There You Are. Jon Kabat-Zinn is a renowned mindfulness teacher, and this book provides a gentle introduction to mindfulness meditation and cultivating awareness in everyday life.

Full Catastrophe Living. In this book, Jon Kabat-Zinn offers a comprehensive guide to his program, mindfulness-based stress reduction (MBSR). It includes practical exercises, guided meditations, and insights into integrating mindfulness into daily life.

Real Happiness: The Power of Meditation. Sharon Salzberg, a meditation teacher, provides a step-by-step guide to meditation, including practices to develop mindfulness, concentration, and compassion.

The Untethered Soul. Michael Singer explores the concept of mindfulness and inner freedom, encouraging readers to let go of limiting thoughts and emotions and embrace the present moment.

The Power of Now. Eckhart Tolle explores living in the present moment and offers practical advice on achieving a state of presence and mindfulness.

Chapter 4

Declutter

"Clutter is not just physical stuff. It's old ideas, toxic relationships, and bad habits. Clutter is anything that does not support your better self."

- ELEANOR BROWNN

"The ability to simplify means to eliminate the unnecessary so that the necessary may speak."

- HANS HOFMANN

DECLUTTERING REFERS TO organizing, simplifying, and streamlining your surroundings by eliminating things that no longer serve a purpose or bring you joy. Decluttering can apply to physical belongings such as clothes, books, furniture, and household items. It can also extend to digital clutter like emails, files, and apps. Additionally, decluttering can involve decluttering your schedule, commitments, and even your mental and emotional "headspace." By letting go of things you no longer need or use, you make space for what truly matters and reduce the psychological and physical burden of extra stuff.

Benefits of Decluttering:
Decluttering has numerous benefits, such as:

- **Reduced Stress and Increased Mental Clarity:** Cluttered spaces can contribute to feelings of overwhelm, stress, and mental fatigue. Decluttering creates a more organized and visually pleasing environment, promoting calmness and clarity and reducing mental and emotional stress.
- **Improved Sleep Quality:** A clutter-free bedroom can create a more relaxing and peaceful atmosphere, promoting better sleep quality. Removing physical clutter from your sleeping space can help reduce anxiety and create an environment conducive to restful sleep.
- **Streamlined Daily Routine:** Decluttering allows you to create efficient systems and organization methods that streamline your daily routines. With everything in its place and easy to find, you can save time and energy in your daily tasks.
- **Enhanced Creativity and Inspiration:** A clutter-free space can stimulate creativity and inspiration. It provides room for new ideas, allows for a clearer thought process, and fosters a sense of mental freedom and openness to new possibilities.

- **Improved Relationships and Social Interactions:** Decluttering can positively impact relationships by creating a more inviting and comfortable environment for spending time with others. It enables you to host guests more comfortably and promotes a sense of pride in your living space.
- **Positive Emotional Well-being:** A clutter-free environment helps create a sense of order, control, and serenity, reducing anxiety, increasing satisfaction, and supporting a sense of contentment.
- **Increased Productivity and Efficiency:** You can work more efficiently and effectively when your workspace is clutter-free. You spend less time searching for items, have fewer distractions, and can focus better on the task at hand, leading to increased productivity.
- **Enhanced Concentration and Focus:** Decluttering helps eliminate visual distractions and allows you to direct your attention and focus more effectively. With a clear and organized space, you can concentrate on tasks, study, or work without clutter's constant visual and mental interference.
- **Enhanced Decision-Making:** Clutter can contribute to decision fatigue and make decision-making more challenging. Decluttering helps simplify choices and reduces the mental burden of managing excessive possessions.

Myths and Misunderstandings about Decluttering

How many of these myths and misunderstandings are familiar to you?

Myth: Decluttering means getting rid of everything.

Reality: Decluttering is about letting go of items or commitments that no longer serve you, but it doesn't necessarily mean getting rid of everything. Decluttering doesn't require that you be a minimalist. While minimalism emphasizes living with few possessions, decluttering can be tailored to your preferences and lifestyle. You can declutter while maintaining a level of possessions that brings you comfort and happiness.

Myth: Decluttering is a one-time event.

Reality: Decluttering is an ongoing process. It's not a one-time task but a habit that involves regularly evaluating and reorganizing your belongings, commitments, and mental/emotional space. Maintenance is required to prevent clutter from accumulating again.

Myth: Decluttering is only about physical possessions.

Reality: Decluttering can extend beyond material possessions to encompass your schedule, commitments, digital clutter, and even your mental and emotional space. However, you don't have to tackle all areas of your life to benefit from decluttering.

Myth: Decluttering is a quick fix for all your problems.

Reality: Decluttering can create a more organized and peaceful environment, schedule, or headspace, but it's not a magical solution to all your problems. It's a step towards a simpler and more intentional lifestyle; other aspects like self-care, personal growth, and mindset shifts may be needed for lasting change.

Myth: Decluttering is a purely physical process.

Reality: Decluttering can have an emotional component. Letting go of items or commitments can evoke big feelings and attachments. It's important to address the emotional aspects and be mindful of your feelings throughout the process.

Myth: Decluttering is about perfection and having a pristine space.

Reality: Decluttering is about creating a space that works for you, not about achieving perfection. It's about finding a level of organization and order that supports your well-being and reduces stress, but it doesn't have to be flawless or match anyone else's standards.

Decluttering Self-Assessment

To assess what areas of your life might need de-cluttering, reflect on the following questions:

1. Are there any activities or commitments on my schedule that no longer bring me joy or serve my priorities?
2. Are there any commitments or obligations I have taken on out of guilt or a sense of obligation rather than genuine interest or alignment with my values?

3. Are there any commitments that I can delegate or let go of to create more space and freedom in my life?
4. Are my commitments aligned with my long-term goals and aspirations?
5. Am I holding onto grudges, regrets, or negative beliefs that are weighing me down?
6. Have I established healthy boundaries to protect my mental and emotional well-being?
7. Have I removed unnecessary and unappealing possessions from my living space?
8. Do I have designated spaces and organizational systems in place for my belongings?
9. Can I easily find and access the things I need without feeling overwhelmed?

Improving Your Ability to Declutter

Decluttering emotional commitments or obligations can be just as important as decluttering physical possessions. Here are some suggestions for tackling both:

- **Work with Your Priorities:** Determine your top priorities and values in life. Consider which emotional commitments and obligations are aligned with your values, and which ones may be causing you stress or overwhelm.
- **Set Boundaries:** Learn to set clear and healthy boundaries with others. Communicate your limits and be assertive about what you can realistically take on. It's essential to strike a balance between helping others and taking care of your own well-being.

- **Assess Relationships:** Evaluate the relationships associated with emotional commitments. Are they mutually supportive and fulfilling, or are they draining and one-sided?
- **Say No:** It's okay to say no when necessary. Politely decline new commitments or requests if you feel overwhelmed or believe they do not align with your priorities.
- **Identify Problematic Spaces:** Focus on spaces that are causing you the most stress or have the most clutter. Spend less time in those spaces. Another approach would be to declutter them.
- **Remove Broken or Unused Items:** Broken or unused items can distract you and cloud your thinking. They symbolize clutter and disorganization. Reduce them.
- **Sort and Categorize Your Physical Clutter:** Divide items into categories like keep, donate, recycle, or discard. This process can help you make decisions more easily.
- **Make Decluttering a Regular Habit:** Implement daily or weekly routines to prevent clutter from accumulating again.

Books about Decluttering

The following books can provide valuable guidance, tips, and inspiration to help you declutter.

Cluttered Mess to Organized Success Workbook: Declutter and Organize Your Home and Life with over 100 Checklists and Worksheets. Cassandra Aarssen's workbook provides practical exercises, checklists, and worksheets to guide you through decluttering and organizing various areas of your life.

Clear Your Clutter with Feng Shui. Karen Kingston combines decluttering principles with the ancient practice of Feng Shui, offering insights into how clutter affects energy flow and providing techniques for creating a harmonious and clutter-free environment.

Unstuff Your Life!: Kick the Clutter Habit and Completely Organize Your Life for Good. Andrew J. Mellen provides guidance on decluttering and organizing various aspects of life, including physical spaces, time management, digital clutter, and more.

Declutter Your Mind: How to Stop Worrying, Relieve Anxiety, and Eliminate Negative Thinking. S.J. Scott and Barrie Davenport focus on decluttering your mental space by addressing negative thinking patterns, reducing anxiety, and developing a clearer and more peaceful mind.

Chapter 5

Manage Stress

"It's not stress that kills us; it is our reaction to it."
                                        - Hans Selye

"Your mind will answer most questions if you learn to relax and wait for the answer."
                                        - William S. Burroughs

Stress is a natural response to challenging or threatening situations. Stressful experiences trigger the body's "fight-or-flight" response, releasing hormones like cortisol and adrenaline. Not all stress is detrimental, but excessive or prolonged stress can negatively impact our physical and mental health.

Stress management practices aim to reduce the negative impacts of stress. They encompass many strategies, including the following:

- Mindfulness and meditation.
- Physical activities like aerobic exercises, strength training, yoga, or walking.
- Relaxation techniques, such as deep breathing exercises, progressive muscle relaxation, guided imagery, or taking warm baths.
- Time management, prioritizing tasks, setting realistic goals, and allocating time for self-care and relaxation.
- Maintaining strong social connections and seeking support by sharing feelings, concerns, and experiences with others.
- Adopting and maintaining healthy lifestyle habits such as getting sufficient sleep, maintaining a balanced diet, limiting caffeine and alcohol intake, and avoiding excessive use of substances like tobacco or recreational drugs
- Carving out time for activities you enjoy, such as hobbies, reading, spending time in nature, volunteering, or engaging in creative pursuits.

Benefits of Stress Management

Stress management has numerous benefits, including:

- **Increased Resilience:** Engaging in stress management practices helps you be more equipped to handle challenging situations, bounce back from setbacks, and maintain a balanced perspective during stressful times.
- **Reduced Physical Symptoms of Stress:** Stress management techniques can reduce physical symptoms

associated with stress, such as tension headaches, muscle aches, and digestive issues.

- **Better Sleep Quality:** Stress management techniques enable more restful and rejuvenating sleep by helping to relax the body and mind, reduce racing thoughts, and release physical tension.
- **Improved Mood:** Stress management supports greater calmness, increased emotional resilience, and improved mood regulation, helping you be better equipped to handle daily challenges.
- **Reduced Need for Unhealthy Coping Strategies:** Coping strategies like avoidance or substance abuse are common responses to chronic stress. Healthier coping mechanisms, such as deep breathing and seeking social support, make us less reliant upon unhealthy strategies.
- **Positive Impact on Relationships:** Effective stress management can lead to improved communication, increased patience, and a better ability to manage conflicts or stressors within your relationships.

Stress Management Myths and Misunderstandings

There are numerous myths and misunderstandings about stress management:

Myth: Avoiding stress is the best approach.

Reality: It's impossible to avoid stress altogether. Stress is a normal part of life and a natural response to challenging situations. Instead of trying to avoid stress altogether, consider developing effective coping mechanisms to manage stress when it arises.

Myth: Stress is always harmful.

Reality: Not all stress is bad. Moderate stress levels, known as "eustress," can motivate and improve performance and productivity. However, excessive and chronic stress, known as "distress," is the type of stress that can have adverse effects on physical and mental health. Learning to identify and address distress is a healthy focus.

Myth: Stress management techniques work the same for everyone.

Reality: People have different responses to stress and varied coping mechanisms that work for them. It's essential to find personalized stress management techniques that resonate with you, considering factors such as your personality, lifestyle, preferences, and strengths.

Myth: Stress management is solely about relaxation techniques.

Reality: While relaxation techniques like deep breathing, meditation, and yoga can be helpful, stress management encompasses a broader range of strategies. It involves embracing a holistic approach that includes regular exercise, healthy eating habits, sufficient sleep, social support, time management, adopting realistic goals, problem-solving, and seeking professional help when necessary.

Myth: Alcohol and substances can effectively reduce stress.

Reality: While substances like alcohol may provide temporary relief, they are not effective as long-term solutions for managing stress. Relying on substances to cope with stress can lead to addiction, worsen mental health issues, and create other problems. Developing healthier coping mechanisms and seeking support from friends, family, or professionals is more beneficial and sustainable.

Stress Management Self-Assessment

To assess your stress management practices, ask yourself the following questions:

1. Do I have stress-management techniques I feel comfortable with and can do regularly?
2. Is my current practice of stress-management techniques sufficient to manage my stress levels and build resilience?
3. Can I practice some techniques more often or more consistently?
4. Can I add some new stress management techniques to my practice?

Improving Your Ability to Practice Stress Management

There are a variety of potential skills involved in stress management.

- **Self-awareness:** Knowing your emotions, thoughts, and physical sensations can help you recognize when stress builds up and take appropriate actions to manage it effectively.

- **Relaxation techniques**: Learning and practicing relaxation techniques such as deep breathing, meditation, progressive muscle relaxation, or guided imagery can help calm the mind and body, reducing stress levels.
- **Time management**: Developing skills in organizing and prioritizing tasks, setting realistic goals, and managing your time effectively can reduce stress caused by feeling overwhelmed or constantly rushed.
- **Problem-solving**: Enhancing your problem-solving skills allows you to approach stressful situations with a proactive mindset. Identifying solutions, evaluating alternatives, and taking action can help reduce stress and improve outcomes.
- **Assertiveness**: Being able to express your needs, set boundaries, and communicate effectively can prevent stress from building up due to conflicts, unrealistic demands, or feeling overwhelmed by others' expectations.
- **Cognitive reframing**: This skill involves challenging and changing negative or irrational thoughts contributing to stress. Reframing your thinking patterns more positively and realistically can reduce stress and cultivate a more resilient mindset.
- **Strengthening your social support network**: This skill is evolving with technology and changes to family structures and community bonds. Developing strong connections with supportive individuals can be beneficial in reducing and coping with stress.
- **Adopting a healthy lifestyle**: Skills that help you to exercise regularly, adopt healthy eating habits, get

sufficient sleep, and practice self-care also help you more effectively manage stress.

- **Flexibility and adaptability:** Cultivating a flexible mindset and being adaptable in the face of change or unexpected events can help reduce stress caused by rigid expectations and increase resilience in challenging situations.

- **Emotional regulation:** Developing skills to identify, understand, and manage your emotions can help prevent stress from escalating and enable more balanced responses to stressful circumstances.

Books about Stress Management

The following books provide insight into the nature of stress, why we should learn to manage stress effectively, and valuable guidance, tips, and inspiration to help you achieve your stress management goals.

The Relaxation Response. Herbert Benson and Miriam Z. Klipper offer practical techniques, such as meditation and deep breathing, to induce relaxation and reduce stress.

The Stress Solution: 4 Steps to a Calmer, Happier, Healthier You. Rangan Chatterjee provides a practical, four-step approach to dealing with stress and improving overall well-being. This book combines medical research with lifestyle advice to help readers tackle stress in various aspects of their lives.

The Stress-Proof Brain: Master Your Emotional Response to Stress Using Mindfulness and Neuroplasticity. Melanie Greenberg explores how mindfulness and neuroplasticity can help individuals cope with stress and manage their emotional responses to challenging situations. This book provides practical strategies and insights to rewire the brain for resilience and stress reduction.

Full Catastrophe Living: Using the Wisdom of Your Body and Mind to Face Stress, Pain, and Illness. Jon Kabat-Zinn, the creator of the Mindfulness-Based Stress Reduction (MBSR) program, presents a comprehensive guide to managing stress, pain, and illness through mindfulness. This book explores the mind-body connection and how mindfulness can enhance well-being.

The Upside of Stress: Why Stress Is Good for You, and How to Get Good at It. Kelly McGonigal explains the potential benefits of stress and how changing our mindset can lead to a healthier response to stress. This book offers insights into how stress can enhance performance and personal growth.

Why Zebras Don't Get Ulcers: An Updated Guide to Stress, Stress-Related Diseases, and Coping. Robert Sapolsky delves into stress's physiological and psychological effects on the human body. He explains the evolutionary reasons behind stress responses and how our bodies cope with stress. The book covers various stress-related diseases and coping mechanisms.

The Mayo Clinic Guide to Stress-Free Living. Amit Sood provides a comprehensive guide to reducing stress and improving overall well-being. He covers various stress management techniques and offers practical advice for achieving a more balanced and stress-free life.

Proactive Mental Health Building Block: Connections

Our relationships with friends, family, neighbors, and coworkers are important in determining how long and well we live. From birth, humans cannot survive without regular social interaction. Social isolation is associated with various ailments, including mental health challenges. Most adults count on others to meet a variety of needs. Many of our most fulfilling and joyous experiences are connected to love, friendship, and a sense of belonging.

Not all social connections enhance our mental health. Sometimes, hurtful or toxic relationships undermine our mental health and overall well-being. There are also times when group cultures support unhealthy behavior, such as drug abuse. Some people damaged by these bad experiences prefer to limit their social interactions. Fixing or reducing exposure to harmful social interactions and relationships while pursuing healthy ones can significantly enhance mental health.

Several behaviors and attitudes are valuable in creating and maintaining healthy social connections. The following six chapters examine how time with friends, love, trust, forgiveness, gratitude, kindness, and teamwork can support our well-being and prevent mental health challenges. Although there is substantial overlap, each chapter offers unique proactive mental health strategies.

Research has revealed that healthy relationships provide a wide range of mental health benefits, such as:

- **Reduced Risk of Mental Health Issues:** Strong social connections have been linked to a lower risk of developing mental health disorders such as depression, anxiety, and stress-related conditions. Social support can act as a buffer against the adverse effects of stress and adversity, enhancing an individual's ability to cope with life challenges.

- **Improved Coping Mechanisms:** People with strong social networks tend to develop better coping strategies to help them manage difficult situations more effectively. The presence of supportive friends or family members can provide emotional comfort and practical assistance during times of distress.

- **Enhanced Resilience:** Social connections contribute to greater psychological resilience. When facing setbacks or trauma, individuals with a robust support system are more likely to bounce back and recover more quickly than those who are socially isolated.
- **Effective Emotional Regulation:** Social interactions can lead to positive emotional experiences and help regulate negative emotions. Sharing thoughts and feelings with others can promote self-expression and provide an outlet for emotional release.
- **Sense of Belonging:** Feeling socially connected gives individuals a sense of belonging and acceptance. This feeling of inclusion is essential for maintaining a positive self-image and overall life satisfaction. Maintaining regular social interactions can reduce the likelihood of feeling lonely and disconnected.
- **Neurobiological Effects:** Research has shown that social connections can influence neurobiological processes related to stress regulation and emotional processing. For example, oxytocin, often called the "bonding hormone," is released during social interactions and is associated with feelings of trust and bonding.
- **Longevity and Physical Health:** Strong social connections are linked to increased physical health and longevity. People with robust social networks tend to have lower rates of chronic diseases and are more likely to adopt healthier lifestyle behaviors.
- **Enhanced Therapeutic Outcomes:** In therapeutic settings, social support and group therapy have been

shown to treat various mental health conditions effectively.

- **Effects Across the Lifespan:** The importance of social connections spans different stages of life, from childhood to old age. Children who experience nurturing relationships tend to develop healthier emotional and cognitive skills, while elderly individuals with social support experience better cognitive function and overall well-being.

How Culture Supports or Undermines Connections

There is an epidemic of loneliness and alienation in many parts of the world. These are broad cultural phenomena. Some of us hoped that technologies such as cell phones and social media would bring us closer together, but many people are experiencing fewer face-to-face social interactions. The quality of those virtual connections is less fulfilling from a mental health perspective. Many of these new ways of connecting are amplifying distrust and conflict.

We will hopefully adjust by developing new cultural norms supporting close relationships and kindness. Social networks have made it possible to reach out to those who share hobbies and interests quickly. We need norms for using these new tools to foster face-to-face gatherings. Gone are the days when a family would share one telephone line. Staying connected and making plans is easier. New norms for getting together regularly could supplant the current norm to connect virtually. New norms for mutual assistance could take advantage of communication technologies (such as phone, instant messaging, and email) that expedite our requests.

Chapter 6

Love and Be Loved

"Love and work are the cornerstones of our humanness."
- SIGMUND FREUD

"The only thing we never get enough of is love, and the only thing we never give enough of is love."
- HENRY MILLER

LOVE INVOLVES THE establishment of emotional connections with others. It is a complex interplay of emotions, including affection, compassion, empathy, and care. Love allows individuals to form deep emotional bonds with others, fostering feelings of belonging and support. It encompasses various forms, such as romantic love, familial love, friendship, and compassion for others.

Love is not a fixed state but a dynamic process that requires ongoing nurturing, effort, and commitment. The expression and experience of love can differ across cultures, individuals, and relationships. The ability to love and be loved is a deeply personal and subjective experience.

Here are some common factors influencing the ability to love and be loved:

- **Emotional Availability:** Being emotionally available means being open to experiencing and expressing emotions, including love and affection. Emotionally available individuals tend to be in touch with their feelings, capable of forming deep connections with others, and comfortable expressing and receiving love in return.

- **Empathy and Compassion:** The ability to understand and share the feelings of others, along with a genuine concern for their well-being, determines your capacity to love and be loved.

- **Secure Attachment Style:** A secure attachment style is characterized by a sense of trust, safety, and comfort in relationships. Individuals with a secure attachment style typically have a positive self-image, believe in their worthiness of love, and have confidence in the availability and responsiveness of others. They are more likely to establish and maintain healthy, loving relationships.

- **Emotional Resilience:** Emotional resilience refers to coping with and recovering from challenging or distressing experiences. Emotionally resilient people can more effectively navigate the ups and downs of relationships, communicate effectively during conflict, and maintain a sense of love and connection even in difficult times.

- **Reciprocity and Generosity:** Being able to reciprocate love and show generosity towards others is a sign of the ability to love and be loved. This includes actively demonstrating care, support, and kindness to loved ones and being receptive to their expressions of love and affection.

- **Healthy Self-esteem:** A healthy sense of self-esteem and self-worth is essential for giving and receiving love. If you have a positive self-image and believe in your value, you are more likely to engage in loving relationships and accept love from others.

- **Relationship Satisfaction:** Feeling satisfied and fulfilled in relationships can indicate the ability to love and be loved. When you experience love and connection in your relationships, which bring you joy, support, and a sense of fulfillment, you are more likely to give and receive love.

Benefits of Loving and Being Loved

There are numerous benefits to giving and receiving love:

- Love has been linked to reduced levels of stress. It can decrease feelings of loneliness and isolation. Acts of love often include assistance that reduces or eliminates sources of stress.

- Receiving love can enhance our self-esteem and self-worth. It validates our sense of being valued, appreciated, and deserving of love, which in turn promotes a positive self-image and a greater sense of confidence.

- Love and emotional support from others can increase resilience and improve coping mechanisms during challenging times. Having someone to lean on, share burdens with, and receive comfort from can provide emotional strength and aid in navigating life's difficulties.

- Love in our relationships provides a sense of purpose. Loving relationships provide opportunities for companionship, shared experiences, and mutual growth, enriching our lives and contributing to a sense of fulfillment.

- Being in a loving relationship can positively influence lifestyle choices. Loving partners often encourage and motivate each other to adopt healthier habits like regular exercise and balanced nutrition. Loving relationships can also discourage risk-taking behaviors.

- Love challenges us to grow and develop as individuals. It encourages personal introspection, self-improvement, and the willingness to understand and accommodate the needs and perspectives of others. It helps us build our capacity to form emotional bonds. Love can inspire us to become better versions of ourselves.

Myths and Misunderstandings About Love

Love is subjective and culturally defined, so determining myths or misunderstandings about love is complicated. However, cultural differences have not stopped research psychologists from identifying love-related myths and misunderstandings. The following list offers some insights that are likely true for many people.

Myth: Love is purely a matter of fate or luck.

Reality: Love is a complex interplay of various factors, including personal characteristics, emotional availability, communication skills, and compatibility. While chance encounters can initiate connections, building and maintaining a loving relationship requires effort, understanding, and active participation from both individuals involved.

Myth: True love is effortless.

Reality: Love requires effort and nurturing. While the initial stages of a relationship can feel euphoric and effortless, long-lasting love requires ongoing commitment, effective communication, compromise, and the willingness to work through challenges. Relationships naturally involve ups and downs; investing time and energy is crucial for maintaining a healthy and fulfilling relationship.

Myth: Romantic love completes you or defines your worth.

Reality: Love should complement and enhance your life, but it does not solely define your worth or identity. While love can bring joy and fulfillment, it is essential to have a sense of self-worth, personal goals, and interests outside of romantic relationships.

Myth: Love is enough to sustain a relationship.

Reality: Relationships require more than just love; they demand effective communication, mutual respect, trust, shared values, emotional support, and a willingness to work through conflicts. Developing and maintaining other essential relationship skills and qualities is important to foster strong and lasting connections.

Myth: The capacity to love is fixed and unchangeable.

Reality: The capacity to love and be loved can grow and evolve. Through self-awareness, self-reflection, and personal growth, individuals can develop their ability to give and receive love. Therapy or counseling can also provide valuable insights and tools to enhance emotional awareness, improve relationship skills, and overcome barriers to experiencing love.

Myth: Love is always a positive experience.

Reality: Love can bring immense joy and happiness, but it can also involve pain, vulnerability, and challenges. Not all relationships are healthy or fulfilling; it's important to recognize and address issues such as toxic relationships, codependency, or unhealthy patterns to pursue supportive, respectful, and nourishing love.

Assessing Your Abilities to Love and to Be Loved

Reflecting on your capacity to love and be loved can be a valuable self-exploration process. Here are some questions that can help you gain insights into your ability to love and be loved:

1. How do I feel when I express love or affection to others? Do I feel comfortable and genuine in expressing my emotions?
2. How do I respond when others express love or affection for me? Am I open to receiving love?
3. Am I able to empathize with others and understand their emotions? How do I demonstrate compassion and care for others?
4. How do I handle conflicts and disagreements in relationships? Can I communicate effectively and find resolutions that maintain love and connection?
5. Do I feel secure, trusting, and comfortable forming close emotional bonds with others?
6. Do I have healthy self-esteem and believe I deserve love?
7. Do I prioritize my emotional well-being in relationships? Can I set boundaries and maintain a sense of self while in relationships?
8. How satisfied and fulfilled do I feel in my current relationships? Do they bring me joy, support, and a sense of emotional connection?
9. How do I show love and affection to myself? Do I practice self-love, self-care, and self-compassion?
10. How resilient am I when facing relationship challenges or setbacks? Can I bounce back and maintain love and connection even during challenging times?
11. How do I approach long-term commitment and intimacy in relationships? Am I open to vulnerability and deep emotional connections?
12. What are my past experiences and patterns in relationships? How have they shaped my ability to love and be loved?

Most people have strengths and limitations regarding loving and being loved. The topic of love is greatly influenced by culture and individual expectations. What would be satisfying for one person may be unsuitable for another person.

Improving Your Ability to Love and Be Loved

Here are some strategies to consider:

- **Develop empathy:** Empathy is the ability to understand and share the feelings of others. Practice putting yourself in other people's shoes, actively listening to their perspectives, and validating their emotions. Empathy fosters deeper connections and can strengthen your relationships.
- **Enhance communication skills:** Effective communication is crucial for building and maintaining healthy relationships. Work on improving both your verbal and non-verbal communication skills. Learn to express your thoughts and feelings openly, honestly, and respectfully. Equally important is learning to listen actively and attentively to others.
- **Build emotional awareness:** Love often involves recognizing and managing your own emotions and understanding the feelings of others. It includes skills like self-regulation, empathy, and social awareness. Developing emotional awareness can help you navigate emotional complexities in relationships and effectively respond to others' needs.
- **Cultivate self-love and self-care:** Loving and accepting yourself is fundamental to experiencing love

with others. Practice self-care activities that nourish your physical, mental, and emotional well-being. Set healthy boundaries and engage in activities that bring you joy and fulfillment.

- **Develop and maintain healthy relationships:** Surround yourself with people who support and uplift you, and invest time and effort in those relationships. Strong relationships often evolve into feelings of mutual love.
- **Learn from past experiences:** Reflect on your past relationships and identify patterns or behaviors that may have hindered your ability to love and be loved. Use these insights as learning opportunities to make positive changes and grow in future relationships.
- **Seek professional help if needed:** If you are struggling with deep-seated emotional issues or experiencing persistent relationship challenges, consider seeking the guidance of a therapist or counselor.

Books about Love

The following books provide valuable guidance and inspiration to develop your understanding, skills, and capacity to love and be loved.

The 5 Love Languages: The Secret to Love That Lasts. Gary Chapman's book introduces the concept of love languages, which are the different ways individuals give and receive love. Understanding your and others' love languages can significantly improve your relationships.

The Relationship Cure: A 5-Step Guide to Strengthening Your Marriage, Family, and Friendships. John Gottman presents practical strategies for building and repairing relationships. This book emphasizes the importance of emotional connection, trust, and effective communication.

Hold Me Tight: Seven Conversations for a Lifetime of Love. Sue Johnson presents a practical guide for strengthening relationships through emotional connection. This book focuses on building trust, enhancing communication, and fostering intimacy.

Love Sense: The Revolutionary New Science of Romantic Relationships. Sue Johnson explores the science behind love and relationships, shedding light on the neurobiology of bonding and attachment. She offers practical advice for creating and maintaining loving connections.

Attached: The New Science of Adult Attachment and How It Can Help You Find--and Keep—Love. Amir Levine and Rachel Heller explore attachment theory and its impact on adult relationships. The book helps readers understand their attachment style and provides guidance on building healthy and secure relationships.

The Mastery of Love: A Practical Guide to the Art of Relationship. Don Miguel Ruiz draws from ancient Toltec wisdom to explore love as an art form, offering insights into overcoming fear and transforming relationships into sources of joy and fulfillment.

Love and Awakening: Discovering the Sacred Path of Intimate Relationship. John Welwood explores the intersection of love and spirituality. He delves into relationships' challenges and transformative potential, offering guidance on cultivating authentic and conscious connections.

Chapter 7

Be with Friends

"Good friends help you to find important things when you have lost them... your smile, your hope, and your courage."

- DOE ZANTAMATA

"A friend is one of the nicest things you can have and one of the best things you can be."

- WINNIE THE POOH

FRIENDSHIP IS AN important remedy for feeling lonely, socially isolated, disconnected, and lacking meaningful relationships. Friendship can come in many forms, including:

- **Close Friends/Best Friends.** Deep emotional bonds, trust, and intimacy characterize these relationships. Close friends are typically the people we feel most comfortable with, share our innermost thoughts and feelings with, and rely on for support and companionship.

- **Childhood Friends.** Childhood friends may share a deep understanding of each other's background and history. Even if the frequency of interaction decreases over time, the bond can remain strong.
- **Work/Colleague Friends.** These friendships can provide social support, an understanding of work-related challenges, and a sense of camaraderie. They may involve spending time together during work hours, engaging in professional discussions, and occasionally extending beyond the workplace.
- **Casual Friends.** These friendships often revolve around shared interests or activities, such as being part of the same interest group, sports team, or social circle. While the depth of these friendships may be more limited, they still provide companionship and shared experiences in specific contexts.
- **Online/Internet Friends.** Virtual friendships are formed and maintained primarily through digital communication platforms like social media, online communities, or gaming platforms. These friendships can be based on shared interests, common online spaces, or virtual support networks. Although virtual friends may rarely or never be together in person, they can offer emotional support, connection, and a sense of belonging.
- **Long-Distance Friends.** These friendships often require more effort and intentionality to stay connected, relying on phone calls, video chats, or occasional visits.

Some friendships fall into more than one category. For example, a childhood friend may be a best friend, and you may develop a virtual friendship with someone you work with remotely.

When taking stock of the friendship landscape in your life, it is helpful to consider both the quantity and quality of those relationships. Meaningful and fulfilling friendships are built on genuine connection, trust, and shared experiences. High-quality friendships often require time, meaningful interactions, and engaging activities that strengthen bonds. Some types of friendships require more time and energy, and some can be maintained with less frequent contact.

As important as friendships may be, it is common to de-prioritize these relationships when other responsibilities demand our time and attention. Modern culture can tell us that friendship is frivolous compared to work, family, and other commitments. The challenge is maintaining social connections while allocating time for work, family, and other demands.

The Benefits of Being with Friends

Healthy friendships are good for us. Here are some of the many benefits of spending time with friends:

- **Improved mood**: Engaging in enjoyable activities, sharing laughter, and having meaningful conversations with friends can lift spirits, reduce stress, and increase happiness and joy. Friends can offer a sense of purpose and a distraction from negative thoughts.
- **Increased resilience**: Friends can provide a crucial source of social support during challenging times.

They may offer a listening ear, understanding, and empathy, which can help people cope with stress, navigate challenging situations, and build resilience. Friends can be stress buffers by providing emotional support, advice, and different perspectives.

- **Reduced risk of mental health challenges:** Regular social interactions with friends have been associated with a lower risk of developing mental health conditions such as depression, anxiety, and cognitive decline.

- **Improved self-esteem:** Spending time with friends who provide positive feedback, validation, and encouragement can enhance self-esteem. Engaging in meaningful interactions and feeling valued by friends contributes to a positive self-image, self-worth, and a sense of belonging.

- **Cognitive stimulation and personal growth:** Interacting with friends often involves stimulating conversations, sharing ideas, and learning from one another. Friends can expose you to different viewpoints, experiences, and knowledge, which can broaden your horizons, promote personal growth, and stimulate intellectual curiosity.

- **Increased sense of belonging:** A supportive circle of friends fosters a sense of belonging and connectedness. This feeling of being part of a social network can promote your mental well-being by reducing feelings of isolation and loneliness.

Myths and Misunderstandings About Friendship

There are many types of friendships, and culture plays an important role in determining the nature and acceptability of various friendships. What is valid for one group may not be accurate for another. However, some misunderstandings and myths are common to many cultures.

Myth: Quantity of friends matters more than quality.

Reality: While having many friends may seem desirable, quality is also important. Close, intimate relationships characterized by trust, emotional support, and reciprocity tend to have a significant impact on mental health.

Myth: Social media interactions are an adequate substitute for face-to-face friendships.

Reality: Although social media platforms provide opportunities for social connections, they cannot fully replace the benefits of in-person interactions. Face-to-face friendships offer unique benefits such as clearer communication, physical touch, and shared experiences, which enhance emotional support and overall mental well-being.

Myth: Extroverts benefit more from socializing than introverts.

Reality: Both extroverts and introverts can derive mental health benefits from spending time with friends, albeit in different ways. Extroverts may gain energy and stimulation from social interactions, while introverts may find solace and support in more intimate or one-on-one settings. The key lies in understanding and honoring your own social needs and preferences.

Myth: More socializing is always better for mental health.
Reality: Although regular social interactions generally benefit mental health, finding a balance that aligns with your needs and preferences is important. For some people, excessive socializing can lead to stress, exhaustion, or feelings of overwhelm. Finding a balance between social and alone time is crucial for optimal mental well-being.

Assessing Your Experience of Friendship

The following questions ask about your experience of friendship. They may help identify current strengths and set goals for improving your friendships.

1. How do I generally feel after spending time with my friends? Do I feel uplifted, happier, and more positive?
2. Do my friends provide emotional support and understanding when I need it?
3. Are my friends good listeners who validate my feelings and concerns?
4. Do I feel comfortable sharing my thoughts and emotions with my friends without fear of judgment?
5. Do I feel a sense of belonging and connection when I spend time with my friends?
6. Are my friends reliable and available when I need support or someone to talk to?
7. Do my friends encourage and motivate me to pursue my goals and dreams?

8. Can I rely on my friends for advice and assistance during challenging times?
9. Do interactions with my friends help me alleviate stress and provide a sense of relief?
10. Can I openly discuss my stressors and challenges with my friends?
11. Are my friends a source of comfort and reassurance when I'm feeling overwhelmed?
12. Do my friends inspire me to try new experiences and expand my interests?
13. Do I learn from my friends and gain new perspectives through our conversations?
14. Do my friends challenge me intellectually and encourage personal growth?
15. Are my friendships characterized by trust, mutual respect, and open communication?
16. Do I feel valued and appreciated by my friends?
17. Are my friendships balanced, with both giving and receiving support?
18. Do I feel comfortable setting boundaries and expressing my needs within my friendships?

Improving Your Ability to Create and Strengthen Friendships

Improving friendships involves developing skills and abilities that contribute to more robust and fulfilling relationships. Here are some key skills and abilities to consider:

- **Communication:** Effective communication is essential for building and maintaining friendships. This includes active listening, expressing oneself clearly and honestly, and being open to understanding others' perspectives. Good communication helps foster trust, understanding, and deeper connections.

- **Empathy and Understanding:** Cultivating empathy allows you to understand and relate to your friends' emotions, experiences, and perspectives. Being empathetic helps create a supportive and compassionate environment, strengthens bonds, and fosters deeper connections.

- **Active Support:** Being actively supportive means being there for your friends during both joyful and challenging times. It involves offering a listening ear, emotional support, and genuine care and interest in their well-being. Being supportive builds trust and strengthens the foundation of friendship.

- **Conflict Resolution:** Conflict is inevitable in any relationship, but knowing how to navigate and resolve conflicts in a healthy and constructive manner is crucial. Developing skills in conflict resolution, such as active listening, compromise, and problem-solving, allows for resolving disagreements while maintaining the friendship.

- **Trustworthiness and Reliability:** Being a trustworthy and reliable friend builds a strong foundation for long-lasting friendships. Keeping commitments, being dependable, and maintaining confidentiality are important aspects of building trust. Trustworthiness fosters a sense of safety and security within the friendship.

- **Boundaries and Respect:** Respecting boundaries is essential for healthy friendships. Respecting each other's personal space, opinions, and autonomy promotes mutual respect and creates a healthy dynamic. Being mindful of boundaries and communicating openly about expectations helps establish and maintain a balanced friendship.

- **Positivity and Supportive Attitude:** Cultivating a positive and supportive attitude can greatly enhance friendships. Being uplifting, offering encouragement, and celebrating each other's successes contribute to a positive and joyful atmosphere within the friendship.

- **Flexibility and Adaptability:** Friendships often change and transition as our lives evolve. Being flexible and adaptable in navigating these changes helps maintain the strength of the friendship. Flexibility allows for growth and evolving dynamics while ensuring the friendship remains strong.

- **Reciprocity:** A healthy friendship involves mutual give-and-take. Being mindful of balancing the level of support, attention, and effort within the friendship helps create a mutually beneficial and fulfilling dynamic.

- **Appreciation and Gratitude:** Expressing gratitude and appreciation for your friends fosters a positive atmosphere and reinforces the bond. Recognizing and acknowledging the value they bring to your life strengthens the friendship.

Books about Friendship

Here are a few notable books about the nature of friendship and how to build and maintain strong friendships.

The Art of Friendship: 70 Simple Rules for Making Meaningful Connections. Roger and Sally Horchow provide practical advice and tips for building and nurturing friendships. This book offers insights into fostering deeper connections, maintaining relationships, and overcoming common friendship challenges.

Friendship: Development, Ecology, and Evolution of a Relationship. Daniel Hruschka examines friendship's biological, psychological, and social aspects, exploring its evolutionary significance and impact on individual well-being.

The Friendship Cure: Reconnecting in the Modern World. Kate Leaver examines the impact of modern life on friendships, including the challenges of loneliness and social isolation. This book offers insights into building and maintaining friendships in an age of social media and digital connections.

Frientimacy: How to Deepen Friendships for Lifelong Health and Happiness. Shasta Nelson delves into the importance of meaningful friendships and offers practical guidance on deepening and strengthening those relationships. The book explores the three key friendship requirements—consistency, positivity, and vulnerability—and provides strategies for cultivating them.

The Girls from Ames: A Story of Women and a Forty-Year Friendship. Jeffrey Zaslow tells the story of eleven women who have maintained strong friendships since childhood. It explores the power of long-lasting friendships and their impact on our lives.

Chapter 8

Forgive

"The act of forgiveness takes place in our mind. It has nothing to do with the other person."

- LOUISE HAY

"Forgiveness does not change the past, but it does enlarge the future."

- PAUL BOESE

FORGIVENESS IS A big and nuanced subject. Forgiveness involves acknowledging the hurt, letting go of negative emotions, and developing empathy and compassion toward the offender. Forgiveness does not imply condoning hurtful behavior or forgetting what happened. It is possible to forgive while still recognizing the wrongdoing and setting boundaries to protect oneself from further harm. In addition to forgiving others, we can forgive ourselves for past mistakes or failures.

Various cultures, groups, and individuals can differ on what constitutes an offense and how or if we forgive. For example, forgiveness is granted after an apology in some households, while a gift is required in other households. Some people find forgiveness a sign of weakness, while others see forgiveness as a sign of strength and maturity.

The Benefits of Forgiveness

Several important psychological benefits can result from forgiveness, such as:

- **Reduced psychological distress**: Forgiveness has been linked to lower levels of psychological distress, including symptoms of depression, anxiety, and stress.
- **Enhanced emotional well-being**: Letting go of resentment, anger, and bitterness can contribute to a greater sense of inner peace, contentment, and happiness.
- **Decreased rumination**: Forgiving others can help individuals break free from the cycle of rumination, which involves repetitively dwelling on negative thoughts and feelings related to the offense. By forgiving, individuals can redirect their mental energy towards other aspects of life.
- **Improved self-esteem**: When individuals forgive themselves for past mistakes or failures, they demonstrate self-compassion and self-acceptance, leading to a more positive self-perception and greater self-worth.

- **Reduced hostility and anger:** Forgiveness helps individuals release hostility and anger towards the offender. Holding onto anger can contribute to chronic stress and negative emotions. By forgiving, individuals experience a decrease in hostility.
- **Increased life satisfaction:** Forgiveness is positively associated with overall life satisfaction. When individuals let go of negative emotions and grudges, they can focus on cultivating positive relationships, engaging in meaningful activities, and pursuing personal goals. This shift in mindset contributes to a greater sense of fulfillment and satisfaction with life.
- **Improved interpersonal relationships:** Forgiveness fosters healthier and more satisfying interpersonal relationships. It allows individuals to rebuild trust, improve communication, and promote empathy and understanding.

Myths and Misunderstandings about Forgiveness

Several myths and misunderstandings can interfere with achieving forgiveness.

Myth: Forgiveness means forgetting or condoning the offense

Reality: Forgiveness does not imply denying or justifying the wrongdoing. It involves acknowledging the harm, letting go of negative emotions, and moving toward healing.

Myth: Forgiveness is a sign of weakness

Reality: Some people believe that forgiving others shows weakness or submission. However, forgiveness can be a courageous and empowering act involving strength, resilience, and the ability to transcend pain. It does not diminish a person's self-worth or imply that they are passive in the face of injustice.

Myth: Forgiveness requires reconciliation or restoring the relationship.

Reality: Forgiveness and reconciliation are separate processes. While forgiveness can contribute to the possibility of reconciliation, it does not guarantee it. Reconciliation involves rebuilding trust and repairing the relationship, which may or may not be feasible or appropriate in every situation. It is possible to forgive someone without resuming or maintaining a relationship with them. Boundaries and self-care are essential considerations in the forgiveness process.

Myth: Forgiveness should be immediate.

Reality: Some believe forgiveness should be granted immediately after an offense. However, forgiveness is a personal process that varies in duration and intensity. It may take time to navigate through complex emotions and arrive at a place of genuine forgiveness.

Assessing Forgiveness

The following questions will help you determine how you are doing with forgiveness.

1. Can I let go of grudges and resentment towards those who have hurt me?
2. Do I hold onto negative emotions such as anger, bitterness, or desire for revenge?
3. Can I empathize with the perspectives and experiences of those who have wronged me?
4. How willing am I to consider the context, circumstances, or personal struggles of the person who hurt me?
5. Am I open to reconciling or rebuilding a relationship with the offender if it is appropriate and safe?
6. Do I feel a sense of relief or emotional release when I think about forgiving someone who has harmed me?
7. Have I noticed any changes in my negative emotions or thought patterns as I've worked through the forgiveness process?
8. Can I separate the person who harmed me from their actions, recognizing that they are fallible and capable of change?
9. Can I practice self-compassion and forgive myself for past mistakes or regrets?

Improving Your Ability to Forgive

Are you ready to forgive? Several attitudes and skills are helpful.

- **Reduce the intensity of negative emotions:** Anger, resentment, or bitterness undermines our capacity to forgive. Although forgiveness doesn't require the complete absence of negative emotions, such negativity can undermine our capacity to forgive.

- **Cultivate empathy:** Try to understand the perspective and feelings of the person who hurt you. Put yourself in their shoes and consider the factors that may have influenced their actions. Empathy can open the door to forgiveness by fostering compassion and understanding. Talking to trusted friends, family members, or professionals who can offer different perspectives may be helpful. Sometimes, gaining insights from others can help you see the bigger picture.

- **Practice self-reflection:** Take time to reflect on your own emotions, thoughts, and reactions. Understand how resentment or anger may impact your well-being and relationships. Recognize the benefits of forgiveness for your personal growth and healing.

- **Release expectations:** Let go of the desire for an apology or for the person who hurt you to change their behavior. Understand that forgiveness is not dependent on external factors. Freeing yourself from expectations can empower you to forgive independently and find peace.

- **Engage in self-care:** Prioritize activities promoting emotional and mental well-being. This may include practicing mindfulness, engaging in hobbies, seeking support from loved ones, or engaging in therapy. Taking care of yourself can create a positive foundation for forgiveness.

- **Set boundaries:** Forgiving someone doesn't mean forgetting what happened or allowing them to continue their harmful behavior. Establishing healthy boundaries to protect yourself and prevent further harm is essential. This may include having no relationship with them at all. If appropriate, communicate your limits clearly and assertively.

- **Practice forgiveness exercises**: Engage in forgiveness exercises, such as writing a forgiveness letter (even if you don't send it) or visualizing a scenario where you offer forgiveness. These exercises can help you process your emotions and gradually move towards forgiveness.

Books about Forgiveness

Forgiving is often not easy. These books can provide valuable guidance, tips, and inspiration to enhance your capacity to forgive.

Forgiveness: A Bold Choice for a Peaceful Heart. Robin Casarjian explores the concept of forgiveness and provides practical guidance on cultivating forgiveness, offering insights, stories, and exercises.

Forgiving the Unforgivable. Beverly Flanigan shares stories of forgiveness from survivors of violence, trauma, and betrayal, offering insights and inspiration on how forgiveness can lead to healing and personal growth.

The Art of Forgiveness, Lovingkindness, and Peace. Jack Kornfield explores forgiveness as a transformative practice, weaving together personal stories, Buddhist teachings, and guided meditations.

The Wisdom of Forgiveness: Intimate Conversations and Journeys. The Dalai Lama and Victor Chan delve into the nature of forgiveness and compassion, offering profound insights and personal stories.

Forgive for Good: A Proven Prescription for Health and Happiness. Fred Luskin shares his research-based approach to forgiveness, providing practical techniques and strategies to let go of grudges and find inner peace.

Forgiveness: How to Make Peace with Your Past and Get on with Your Life. Sidney and Suzanne Simon offer a step-by-step guide to forgiveness, providing practical exercises, case studies, and tools to help readers let go of resentment and find freedom.

The Book of Forgiving: The Fourfold Path for Healing Ourselves and Our World. Archbishop Desmond Tutu and his daughter, Mpho Tutu, offer a powerful framework for forgiveness, drawing on personal stories, spiritual teachings, and practical exercises.

Chapter 9

Practice Gratitude

"The more you practice gratitude, the more you see how much there is to be grateful for, and your life becomes an ongoing celebration of joy and happiness."

- LOUISE HAY

"Thank you is the best prayer that anyone could say. I say that one a lot. Thank you expresses extreme gratitude, humility, understanding."

- ALICE WALKER

GRATITUDE INVOLVES SHIFTING your perspective from focusing on what is lacking or negative to recognizing the abundance and positivity in your life. It's about reframing your thoughts and embracing a more positive mindset. Gratitude is not about tolerating unpleasant or unproductive experiences and relationships. It is, however, about noticing pleasant and supportive experiences and relationships. You can be grateful for some aspects of life even while others are not so positive. You can be grateful to someone for their support and kindness even when other acts are less thoughtful.

The Benefits of Gratitude

Practicing gratitude has been found to have a wide range of positive effects, such as:

- **Increased Sense of Well-being:** People who practice gratitude tend to experience higher levels of happiness and life satisfaction. They often report more frequent positive emotions, such as joy, contentment, and optimism. Cultivating gratitude can contribute to a more positive outlook and fulfillment.

- **Reduced Depression and Anxiety:** Research suggests that gratitude is associated with lower levels of depression and anxiety. People who practice gratitude often have a more resilient mindset when facing challenges. Gratitude can help shift focus away from negative thoughts and promote a more positive mental state.

- **Enhanced Resilience:** Gratitude is linked to the ability to bounce back from adversity. People who practice gratitude are better equipped to cope with stress, trauma, and difficult life events. They often display higher levels of emotional strength, adaptability, and an optimistic outlook, enabling them to navigate challenges more effectively.

- **Strengthened Relationships:** Expressing gratitude can enhance relationships. People who practice gratitude tend to engage in more prosocial behaviors, such as acts of kindness, empathy, and support. They experience greater satisfaction in relationships, deeper connections, and increased social support. Gratitude can foster a positive and appreciative atmosphere in personal and professional interactions.
- **Stress Reduction:** Gratitude practices have been shown to reduce stress levels and promote better sleep and relaxation. People who practice gratitude often have lower levels of the stress hormone cortisol, leading to a decreased physiological stress response. Regularly focusing on gratitude can help counteract the negative impact of stress on mental and physical health.
- **Increased Self-esteem:** People who practice gratitude often have a positive self-image and greater self-confidence. By acknowledging and appreciating their and others' contributions, they cultivate a more positive and compassionate view of themselves.

Myths and Misunderstandings about Gratitude

There are several myths and misunderstandings that can interfere with gratitude.

Myth: Gratitude is just about saying "thank you."

Reality: While expressing gratitude through words or actions is an essential aspect of gratitude, it is not limited to the simple act of saying "thank you." Gratitude involves a deeper appreciation and recognition of life's positive aspects, including recognizing personal blessings and being mindful of the present moment.

Myth: Gratitude is only for big or extraordinary things

Reality: Gratitude is not only for monumental or extraordinary events. Appreciating life's small, everyday moments and simple pleasures is equally important. Cultivating gratitude involves recognizing and being thankful for both large and small aspects of our lives.

Myth: Gratitude requires ignoring the negative

Reality: Gratitude is more than just positive thinking or trying to ignore negative experiences. It is a balanced perspective that acknowledges both positive and negative aspects of life while actively choosing to focus on and appreciate the positive. Gratitude does not invalidate or dismiss negative emotions but instead helps to reframe and shift attention toward the positive.

Myth: Gratitude is solely an individual effort

Reality: While gratitude practices often involve personal reflection, gratitude is also a social experience. Expressing gratitude to others and recognizing their contributions is crucial in building and maintaining relationships. Gratitude can strengthen social connections and promote a sense of community and belonging.

Myth: Gratitude is a one-time practice

Reality: Gratitude is most effective when practiced consistently over time. It is not a one-time activity but a mindset and a habit that can be developed through regular practice. Engaging consistently in gratitude exercises, such as keeping a gratitude journal, can help integrate gratitude into daily life.

Gratitude Self-Assessment

These questions will help you see how you are doing with gratitude.

1. What am I grateful for in my life right now?
2. Do I regularly take time to reflect on and appreciate the positive aspects of my life?
3. How often do I notice and express gratitude for the small joys in my daily routine?
4. Do I actively seek opportunities to express my gratitude to others, both close relationships and strangers alike?
5. Do I find things to be grateful for, even in challenging situations?
6. Am I mindful and present enough to fully appreciate the positive experiences as they happen?
7. How often do I thank and appreciate myself for my accomplishments and qualities?

Increasing Your Gratitude Skills and Abilities

Several skills and abilities can enhance gratitude:
- **Mindfulness:** Practice being present and noticing the positive things around you. Pay attention to the small

details and moments that often go unnoticed. Being mindful helps you develop a more profound gratitude for the present moment.

- **Reflection:** Take time to reflect on what you are grateful for. This can include people, experiences, achievements, opportunities, or even the simple joys of life. Become aware of the positive aspects of your life. Gratitude involves recognizing and acknowledging the blessings, kindness, and goodness you experience.

- **Gratitude Expression:** Express gratitude for the things and people you appreciate. This can be done in various ways, such as saying thank you, writing a gratitude journal, or expressing appreciation to others through kind words or gestures. Verbalizing or writing down your gratitude reinforces the positive emotions associated with it. Effective communication skills enable you to express your gratitude to others. Strong communication skills facilitate the expression of gratitude.

- **Empathy:** Empathy is the capacity to understand and share the feelings of others. Putting yourself in someone else's shoes can deepen your appreciation for their actions, contributions, and support, fostering gratitude.

Books about Gratitude

The following books focus on the complex and important relationship between gratitude and mental health. They also explain how and when to practice gratitude.

Grateful: The Transformative Power of Giving Thanks. Diana Butler Bass explores the spiritual dimension of gratitude and its potential to transform our lives. She discusses the connection between gratitude and faith, emphasizing the importance of cultivating a grateful mindset to find meaning, healing, and joy.

The Gratitude Diaries: How a Year Looking on the Bright Side Can Transform Your Life. Janice Kaplan shares her journey of dedicating a year to focus on gratitude and its impact on her life. Through her experiences and interviews with experts, she highlights the transformative power of gratitude in enhancing happiness and overall well-being.

Thanks!: How the New Science of Gratitude Can Make You Happier. Robert Emmons explores the positive effects of gratitude on happiness and offers practical strategies for cultivating gratitude. He delves into the benefits of gratitude practice, its impact on relationships, and its ability to improve mental and physical health.

365 Thank Yous: The Year a Simple Act of Daily Gratitude Changed My Life. John Kralik shares his personal story of writing a thank-you note every day for a year and how this simple act of gratitude transformed his life. He highlights the power of expressing appreciation and its profound impact on relationships, personal growth, and finding happiness.

The Gratitude Jar: A Simple Guide to Creating Miracles. Josie Robinson introduces the concept of the gratitude jar as a tool for cultivating gratitude. The book offers personal stories, practical exercises, and guidance on creating a gratitude jar and using it as a source of inspiration, mindfulness, and transformation in daily life.

Chapter 10

Trust

"Trust is the glue of life. It's the most essential ingredient in effective communication. It's the foundational principle that holds all relationships."

— STEPHEN R. COVEY

"The best way to find out if you can trust somebody is to trust them."

— ERNEST HEMINGWAY

TRUST IS A fundamental belief or confidence placed in someone or something. Being trustworthy means consistently demonstrating qualities and behaviors that inspire others to trust you. There are multiple forms of trust:

- **Contextual trust** means that our relationship has a broad basis of familiarity. As we get to know the history and special interests of others, we can begin to appreciate and trust them more. This trust is sometimes established through years of shared life experiences. This could be true of family members or longtime friends. However, all too often, people spend years working and living side by side without knowing much about the others' range of experiences. At work, for example, we may know our peers' specific tasks or job responsibilities without knowing anything about their family life, hobbies, and personal aspirations.

- **Communication trust** refers to the willingness to disclose relevant information. It also refers to using personal information in a considerate way. Accurate and complete information is also important. If you withhold your true feelings, the quality and quantity of support are undermined. In contrast, when communication trust is high, information flows freely.

- **Contractual trust** is developed when peers agree about how their relationship will function. This doesn't mean that rules are set in stone, but it does mean that the helping relationship will be organized to respect time and other commitments. Creating a schedule, sticking with it, and showing up on time are all examples of how to build contractual trust.

- **Competence trust** involves respecting people's knowledge, skills, abilities, and judgments. To establish this form of trust, you must be clear about your strengths and limitations. For example, you should let someone know if you have little formal training or experience with an issue that has been raised. Frank disclosure of experience (or the lack thereof) enhances competence trust. However, it is insufficient to declare a lack of familiarity, knowledge, or skills. You build competence trust by actively pursuing helpful information.

Culture influences our abilities to trust and be trustworthy. In some cultures, for example, consistently being truthful is a strong norm. In other cultures, fidelity to the leader is more important than sticking with the facts. In such cultures, the ability to be dishonest is required to be trusted with responsibilities. In some highly dysfunctional cultures, trusting and being trustworthy are seen as being naïve and lacking in good judgment. Such cultures are unlikely to achieve levels of trust that support mental health.

The Benefits of Trust

Being able to trust and be trustworthy offers numerous benefits, such as:

- **Strong Relationships:** Trust is the foundation of healthy and meaningful relationships. When you are trustworthy and can trust others, it creates a sense of security, openness, and mutual respect. It allows for deeper connections, fosters effective communication, and strengthens bonds.
- **Effective Collaboration:** Trust is crucial for successful teamwork and collaboration. When team members trust each other, they feel comfortable sharing ideas,

expressing concerns, and taking risks. Trust enhances cooperation, facilitates problem-solving, and leads to higher productivity and innovation within groups or organizations.

- **Enhanced Reputation:** Trustworthy individuals tend to have a positive reputation. Others perceive them as reliable, honest, and dependable, which can lead to greater personal and professional opportunities. Trustworthy individuals often attract more meaningful relationships, job opportunities, and collaborative ventures.

- **Improved Communication:** Trust reduces barriers to communication. When people trust each other, they are likelier to share information openly and honestly. This fosters effective dialogue, encourages active listening, and promotes understanding. Trust allows for constructive feedback and facilitates the resolution of conflicts.

- **Increased Emotional Well-being:** Trusting relationships provide a sense of safety, support, and belonging. When you trust others, you can rely on their support during challenging times, and being trustworthy allows you to build a positive self-image and sense of integrity.

Myths and Misunderstandings About Trust

The following myths and misunderstandings can interfere with trust.

Myth: Trust is blind and unconditional.

Reality: Trust is neither blind nor unconditional. Trust is developed based on past experiences, observations, and ongoing interactions. It is influenced by evidence of reliability, honesty, and consistency in the behavior of others.

Myth: Once broken, trust can never be repaired.

Reality: Although betrayal can damage trust, trust can sometimes be repaired. Rebuilding trust requires effort, open communication, and consistent, trustworthy behavior. Trust may be restored with sincere apologies, reparative actions, and mutual commitment.

Myth: Trustworthiness is solely about keeping promises.

Reality: Trustworthiness encompasses more than just keeping promises. It involves consistently displaying integrity, honesty, and dependability in various aspects of life.

Myth: To trust others is to be gullible.

Reality: Trust is not synonymous with gullibility. Trust involves a rational assessment of others based on available information and experiences. Conversely, gullibility is a naive and indiscriminate tendency to trust without proper evaluation, leading to vulnerability.

Myth: Trust is solely an individual characteristic.

Reality: Trust is a two-way process influenced by individual characteristics and contextual factors. Trust is shaped by personal beliefs, experiences, and cultural norms, as well as the behaviors and reputations of others. Trust is a dynamic interaction between individuals and their cultural environment.

Myth: Trustworthiness requires perfection.

Reality: Trustworthiness does not mean being perfect or never making mistakes. Everyone is fallible. Trustworthy individuals acknowledge their mistakes, take responsibility, and work towards rectifying them. Trust is built on a foundation of honesty and accountability.

Myth: Trust is solely based on intuition or gut feeling.

Reality: Although intuition can play a role in forging trust, it is not the sole determinant. Trust is a complex process influenced by various cognitive, emotional, and social factors. Rational assessments, observations, and evidence-based judgments also contribute to developing trust.

Myth: Trust can be demanded or forced.

Reality: Trust must be earned; it develops over time through consistent, trustworthy behavior. Merely insisting on trust without demonstrating trustworthiness is unlikely to be effective and may even lead to skepticism or distrust.

Trust Self-Assessment

These questions can help you assess your ability to trust others:

1. How willing am I to be open and vulnerable with others?
2. Do I generally give others the benefit of the doubt, or do I find it challenging to trust people?
3. Have past experiences of betrayal or disappointment affected my ability to trust others?
4. How do I evaluate and assess the reliability and credibility of others before deciding to trust them?
5. Am I comfortable with uncertainty and taking risks in relationships?
6. Do I tend to have a balanced level of skepticism, neither unquestioningly trusting nor overly suspicious?
7. How do I respond to situations where trust is required? Do I approach them with an open mind or with guarded skepticism?

To assess your ability to be trustworthy:

1. How consistently do I keep my promises and fulfill commitments?
2. Do I act with integrity and honesty in my life?
3. How reliable and consistent am I in my behavior and actions towards others?
4. Do I respect others' boundaries and keep confidential information private?
5. Am I accountable for my actions and willing to apologize and make amends when I make mistakes?
6. How do I handle ethical dilemmas, and do I prioritize treating others fairly?
7. How do I handle situations where my interests may conflict with the trust placed in me by others?

Increasing Your Capacity to Trust and Be Trusted

Several skills and abilities help cultivate trust.

- **Effective Communication:** Develop strong communication skills, both verbal and non-verbal. This includes active listening, clearly expressing thoughts and feelings, and conveying information honestly and respectfully.

- **Honesty and Integrity:** Cultivate a personal commitment to honesty and integrity in all your actions. Be truthful and reliable, follow through on your promises, and uphold high ethical standards.

- **Emotional Control:** Don't lose your cool. Understand and manage your own emotions effectively. Avoid intentionally hurtful or thoughtless responses.

- **Reliability and Accountability:** Be dependable and consistent in your actions and commitments. Take responsibility for your own mistakes and learn from them. When you make promises or commitments, ensure that you follow through on them.

- **Active Trust:** Practice actively trusting others until they give you a reason not to. Give others the benefit of the doubt and assume positive intent. This doesn't mean being naive or unquestioningly trusting everyone, but instead starting with a baseline level of trust and adjusting it based on evidence.

- **Empowerment and Delegation:** Learn to delegate tasks and responsibilities to others, empowering them to take ownership. This demonstrates trust in their abilities.

- **Conflict Resolution:** Develop skills in resolving conflict constructively and fairly. Seek win-win solutions, listen to different perspectives, and work towards understanding and compromise.
- **Boundaries and Respect:** Establish and communicate your boundaries while respecting the boundaries of others. This creates a sense of safety and trust in relationships.
- **Patience and Forgiveness:** Practice patience and be willing to forgive others for their mistakes. Trust takes time to build and can be fragile, but it can also be repaired with genuine effort and forgiveness.

Books about Trust

The following books help to define trust, explain its many benefits, and how it can be strengthened.

Who Can You Trust?: How Technology Brought Us Together and Why It Might Drive Us Apart. Rachel Botsman explores the changing dynamics of trust in the digital age and discusses the implications of technology on trust in various aspects of life.

The Speed of Trust: The One Thing That Changes Everything. Stephen Covey explores the importance of trust in personal and professional relationships and provides practical strategies for building and maintaining trust.

Trust: Human Nature and the Reconstitution of Social Order. Francis Fukuyama explores the concept of trust from a societal perspective, examining its role in building strong institutions and fostering social cooperation.

Trust: Self-Interest and the Common Good. Marek Kohn explores trust from a psychological and sociological perspective, examining the factors influencing trust in society and its impact on individuals and communities.

Trust and Betrayal in the Workplace: Building Effective Relationships in Your Organization. Dennis and Michelle Reina offer frameworks, examples, and actionable advice to help individuals and organizations build a culture of trust.

The Psychology of Trust. Kenneth Rotenberghis comprehensively examines the psychological aspects of trust, exploring its development, maintenance, and effects on individuals and relationships.

Building Trust: In Business, Politics, Relationships, and Life. Robert Solomon and Fernando Flores offer insights into the nature of trust, its importance, and practical advice for developing trust in various areas of life.

Trust and Conflict: Representation, Culture, and Dialogue. Editors Peter Steinberger and Vincent Geoghegan explore the relationship between trust and conflict, examining how trust can influence conflict resolution and negotiation processes from a psychological perspective.

Chapter 11

Team Up

"Alone, we can do so little; together, we can do so much."
- HELEN KELLER

"Teamwork is the ability to work together toward a common vision.
- ANDREW CARNEGIE

TEAMWORK IS THE collaborative effort of a group of individuals working together to achieve a common goal or complete a shared task. In workplaces, there are project teams, departmental teams, or cross-functional teams. Outside of work, collaboration is important to the success of families, sports teams, support groups, online communities, and civic organizations.

Key characteristics of effective teamwork include:

- **Cooperation:** Team members actively cooperate, communicate, and coordinate their efforts to accomplish the task at hand.
- **Shared Goals:** The team shares a common purpose and objective, which serves as the driving force behind their actions.
- **Interdependence:** Each team member's contributions affect and rely on the contributions of others, promoting mutual support.
- **Communication:** Open and effective communication is crucial for sharing ideas, discussing progress, and resolving conflicts.
- **Support and Trust:** Team members trust one another and provide support, fostering a positive and encouraging environment.
- **Division of Labor:** Tasks are distributed based on individual strengths and skills, ensuring that the right people are responsible for specific aspects of the project.
- **Problem-Solving:** Teams collaboratively address challenges, brainstorm solutions, and make decisions collectively.
- **Accountability:** Each team member takes responsibility for their actions and commitments, promoting a sense of ownership and dedication to the team's success.
- **Flexibility:** Teams are adaptive and open to change, allowing them to respond effectively to evolving circumstances.
- **Recognition of Diversity:** Diverse perspectives and backgrounds contribute to innovation and creativity within a team.

Culture affects if and how we form teams. Due to its emphasis on the individual, American culture can sometimes discourage teamwork. In such highly individualistic cultures, which value competition, people must overcome discomfort with collaboration to form effective teams. In more collaborative cultures, on the other hand, teams must work to overcome the tendency to overlook individual perspectives. In such cultures, group thinking and the desire to fit in can overwhelm the contributions of individuals.

The Benefits of Teamwork

Engaging in effective teamwork can have positive impacts on individuals' mental well-being. Here are a few notable benefits:

- **Reduced stress and improved resilience:** Teamwork fosters a supportive and collaborative environment where individuals can share responsibilities, rely on one another, and provide emotional support. This shared responsibility and support network can help distribute stress and workload, reducing individual stress levels. Additionally, when teams face challenges and work collectively to overcome them, it can enhance resilience, allowing individuals to cope better with stressors.

- **Accountability and follow-through:** Effective teams encourage their members to stay focused and on track. The emotional and instrumental support teammates provide to each other makes it easier to tackle challenging goals and overcome adversity.

- **Increased sense of belonging and connection:** Being part of a well-functioning team provides a sense of belonging and social connection. Humans are social beings. Meaningful relationships with others are important for mental well-being. Good teamwork creates a supportive and cohesive group dynamic where individuals feel valued, accepted, and understood. This sense of belonging can contribute to higher self-esteem and overall life satisfaction.

- **Enhanced self-efficacy and confidence:** Working effectively within a team can boost peoples' self-efficacy, which refers to their belief in their abilities to achieve goals and handle challenges. When team members successfully collaborate, solve problems together, and contribute their unique skills, it reinforces their confidence in their abilities. This increased self-efficacy can positively spill over to other areas of life, improving mental well-being.

- **Improved communication and interpersonal skills:** Effective teamwork involves open and constructive communication, active listening, and understanding and empathizing. These skills facilitate better teamwork and can improve personal and professional relationships.

- **Sense of achievement:** Accomplishing team goals and experiencing success together can provide a sense of accomplishment and fulfillment. Team members often share in the joy of accomplishing objectives, which can boost motivation and satisfaction. This sense of accomplishment and motivation can positively influence individuals' mental well-being by promoting a sense of purpose, self-worth, and inspiration to pursue further challenges.

Myths and Misunderstandings about Teamwork

There are several myths and misunderstandings that can interfere with teamwork.

Myth: Teamwork means everyone always agrees with each other.

Reality: While consensus is desirable in some situations, effective teamwork does not always require unanimous agreement. Constructive disagreements and diverse perspectives can lead to better decision-making and innovation. Healthy debates and discussions allow teams to consider different viewpoints, challenge assumptions, and arrive at well-informed conclusions.

Myth: Strong teams are made up of individuals with similar skills and personalities.

Reality: While it may be tempting to form teams with individuals with similar skills and personalities, research suggests that diverse groups tend to perform better. Diverse teams bring various perspectives, knowledge, and problem-solving approaches, which can enhance creativity, decision-making, and overall team performance.

Myth: Teamwork means everyone has an equal say and contributes equally.

Reality: Equal contribution and input from all team members may not always be practical or necessary for effective teamwork. Each team member brings unique strengths and expertise, and their contributions may vary based on the task or context. It is essential to recognize and leverage individual strengths while ensuring that everyone has opportunities to contribute and be heard.

Myth: The most successful teams have the highest individual talent or intelligence.

Reality: Although individual talent and intelligence are valuable, they are not the sole determinants of team success. Effective teamwork goes beyond individual abilities. Factors such as communication, collaboration, trust, and shared goals play significant roles in team performance. A team with members who excel in these interpersonal and collaborative skills can outperform a group with high individual talent but poor teamwork abilities.

Myth: Teamwork always leads to positive outcomes.

Reality: Although teamwork can be highly beneficial, it does not guarantee success in every situation. Teams may encounter challenges, conflicts, and setbacks along the way. Effective teams are resilient, adaptable, learn from failures, and use them as opportunities for growth. Overcoming obstacles and setbacks can ultimately strengthen the team and contribute to long-term success.

Teamwork Self-Assessment

These questions will help you reflect on various aspects of teamwork and provide insights into your strengths, weaknesses, and areas for improvement:

1. Do I actively listen to my teammates and consider their perspectives?
2. Can I express my ideas and opinions clearly and effectively?
3. Do I provide constructive feedback and actively contribute to discussions?
4. How well do I contribute my skills and expertise to achieve team goals?
5. Do I seek opportunities to support and assist my teammates when needed?
6. How well do I handle conflicts or disagreements within a team?
7. How do I manage my emotions and maintain positive relationships during conflict?
8. Am I open to new ideas and approaches suggested by my teammates?
9. Am I respectful and considerate of my teammates' opinions and contributions?
10. Do I recognize and appreciate the diverse strengths and perspectives within a team?
11. Can I effectively follow the lead of others when necessary?
12. How do I contribute to creating a cohesive and motivated team?

Skills and Abilities for Enhanced Teamwork

You can significantly enhance your effectiveness in a team setting by cultivating practical abilities such as these:

- **Join or Create Groups or Teams:** Teamwork requires practice. Join or create a team so that you can learn how to build teams and engage in activities that strengthen relationships and enhance cooperation within the group. You can learn from how others enhance and undermine teamwork.

- **Communication:** Practice active listening, be clear and concise in your speech, and encourage open and honest dialogue with your team members. Avoid making assumptions and always seek clarification when needed.

- **Build Trust:** Be reliable, keep promises, and support your teammates. Avoid gossip and confront conflicts constructively and respectfully.

- **Recognize and Utilize Strengths:** Acknowledge the strengths of others and utilize them to your advantage. Assign tasks based on individual expertise and encourage collaboration to maximize the team's potential.

- **Be a Team Player:** Demonstrate a positive and cooperative attitude. Be willing to help others, share credit for successes, and take responsibility for mistakes. Avoid seeking personal glory at the expense of others.

- **Set Clear Goals and Roles:** Establish clear objectives for the team and ensure everyone understands their roles and responsibilities. Regularly assess progress and adjust as necessary.

- **Adaptability and Flexibility:** Be open to new ideas and approaches. Adaptability is essential in dynamic team environments.
- **Manage Conflict Constructively:** Conflict is a natural part of teamwork but can be detrimental if not handled properly. Learn how to manage disagreements and conflicts constructively by staying calm, understanding different perspectives, and finding compromises.
- **Embrace Diversity and Inclusion:** Value and respect the diversity of your team members. Embrace different perspectives and experiences, as they can lead to innovative solutions and richer discussions.
- **Celebrate Achievements:** Acknowledge and celebrate both individual and team achievements. Recognition and positive reinforcement boost team morale and foster a sense of accomplishment.
- **Continuous Learning:** Be open to learning from your experiences and seek feedback from teammates and supervisors. Continuous improvement is vital for personal growth and effective teamwork.

Books about Teamwork

The following books provide valuable guidance, tips, and inspiration to enhance your capacity to engage in teamwork.

Quiet: The Power of Introverts in a World That Can't Stop Talking. Susan Cain explores the strengths and contributions of introverts in teamwork and highlights the value of creating environments that accommodate different personality types.

The Culture Code: The Secrets of Highly Successful Groups. Daniel Coyle uncovers the key components that contribute to cohesive and high-performing teams. This book explores the importance of safety, vulnerability, and shared purpose.

The Ideal Team Player: How to Recognize and Cultivate the Three Essential Virtues. Patrick Lencioni focuses on three virtues that make individuals effective team players: humility, hunger, and people smarts. Lencioni provides practical guidance on identifying and developing these qualities in team members.

Collaborative Intelligence: Thinking with People Who Think Differently. Dawna Markova and Angie McArthur explore how diverse perspectives can lead to breakthrough innovations and enhanced team performance. This book offers tools and techniques to tap into the collective intelligence of teams.

Group Genius: The Creative Power of Collaboration. Keith Sawyer examines the science of creativity in group settings, exploring how individuals can work together to generate innovative ideas and solutions.

Chapter 12

Be Kind

"Kindness is the only service that will stand the storm of life and not wash out."

\- ABRAHAM LINCOLN

"Kindness in words creates confidence. Kindness in thinking creates profoundness. Kindness in giving creates love."

\- LAO TZU

KINDNESS IS CONSIDERATE and benevolent intentions and actions. It involves caring, empathy, and understanding other people's feelings, needs, and circumstances. Kindness goes beyond superficial gestures and involves a sincere desire to make a positive difference in someone's life.

Although kindness often refers to how others are treated, it also applies to how to treat yourself. Self-kindness involves treating yourself with the same warmth, understanding, and care you would offer a friend or loved one. It means recognizing your worth and treating yourself with empathy, especially during challenging times.

Kindness has many faces. Here are some qualities of kindness:

- **Empathy:** Kindness involves understanding the feelings and perspectives of others. This understanding helps guide thoughtful responses and helpful actions.
- **Compassion:** Kindness involves showing concern and care for the well-being of others. Compassionate individuals are motivated to alleviate suffering and offer support when needed.
- **Generosity:** Kindness often involves giving freely.
- **Altruism:** Kindness is driven by a genuine desire to help regardless of potential personal benefit.
- **Consistency:** Kindness is not a matter of convenience. It is about a commitment to treating people with compassion and care, even in challenging circumstances.
- **Respect:** Kindness involves treating people with respect and dignity, regardless of their background, beliefs, or circumstances. It embraces diversity and seeks to create a sense of belonging for all individuals.
- **Sincerity:** Kindness is not merely performative but is deeply felt and expressed.
- **Patience:** Kindness often requires patience, especially when dealing with challenging situations or people.

- **Forgiveness:** An act of kindness can include forgiving and letting go of past grievances.
- **Assumption of positive intent:** Kindness involves assuming positive intent and giving people the benefit of the doubt.

The Benefits of Kindness

Engaging in acts of kindness and cultivating a kind attitude can have significant positive effects on mental health, including:

- **Reduced stress:** Acts of kindness, both giving and receiving, have been shown to lower stress levels. Engaging in kind behaviors can activate the release of hormones like oxytocin, which helps reduce stress and anxiety.
- **Increased happiness:** Performing acts of kindness is associated with increased positive emotions and happiness. Kindness triggers the release of neurotransmitters like dopamine and endorphins, which contribute to a better mood and overall well-being.
- **Improved self-esteem:** Being kind to others and oneself can boost self-esteem and self-worth. Engaging in acts of kindness can create a sense of purpose and meaning, leading to a more positive self-perception.
- **Enhanced social connections:** Kindness fosters positive social interactions and strengthens social bonds, leading to a greater sense of belonging and social support.
- **Reduced feelings of isolation:** Kindness can help combat loneliness and isolation.

- **Reduced symptoms of depression:** Some studies have found that engaging in acts of kindness is associated with a reduction in symptoms of depression. Kindness can counteract negative thoughts and emotions, contributing to improved mental well-being.
- **Increased life satisfaction:** Kindness and prosocial behavior are linked to greater fulfillment and purpose.
- **Enhanced resilience:** Kindness can contribute to increased resilience, the ability to bounce back from adversity, and effectively cope with life's challenges. Engaging in acts of kindness can provide individuals with a sense of purpose and motivation during difficult times.
- **Lowered levels of anger and hostility:** Engaging in acts of kindness can help reduce feelings of anger and hostility. Kindness and empathy can promote a more positive and compassionate outlook on life.

Myths and Misunderstandings about Kindness

There are several myths and misunderstandings about kindness:

Myth: Kindness is a sign of weakness.

Reality: Kindness is not synonymous with being a pushover. Kindness can coexist with assertiveness and healthy boundaries.

Myth: Kindness requires grand gestures:

Reality: Although big acts of kindness may be impactful, kindness is not limited to grand gestures. Small acts of kindness in everyday interactions can have a significant positive effect.

Myth: Kindness is always reciprocated.
Reality: Although sometimes reciprocal, kindness does not depend on reciprocity.

Myth: Kindness is innate; you can't learn it.
Reality: Kindness is both innate and learned. Although some people may have a natural inclination towards kindness, it is a skill that can be cultivated and nurtured through practice and intention.

Myth: Kindness means saying "yes" to everything.
Reality: Kindness does not mean always saying "yes" to every request or demand. Balancing kindness with self-care and the ability to say "no" when necessary is essential; sustainable kindness requires healthy boundaries.

Myth: Kindness is only about others.
Reality: Kindness should extend to ourselves as well. Self-kindness is essential for maintaining overall well-being and effectively showing kindness to others.

Myth: Kindness is effortless.
Reality: Kindness may come naturally to some individuals, but genuine kindness often requires effort and intention. It

involves considering others' needs, emotions, and perspectives, as well as our abilities and capacity.

Myth: Kindness is always gentle and soft-spoken.

Reality: Kindness can be expressed in various ways, including assertiveness and advocating for what is right. Standing up against injustice and promoting equality can also be acts of kindness.

Myth: Kindness is only about doing good deeds.

Reality: Kindness also involves the way we think and speak about others. Cultivating kind thoughts and words is as important as performing kind actions.

Myth: Kindness means avoiding confrontation.

Reality: Kindness does not equate to avoiding necessary confrontations or difficult conversations. It is possible to address conflicts kindly, with empathy and respect.

Kindness Self-Assessment

Answering the following questions can help determine how you are doing with kindness.

1. How do I typically respond when someone asks for help or support?
2. Do I actively seek opportunities to perform acts of kindness or wait for others to initiate them?

3. How do I feel when I witness acts of kindness in others? Does it inspire me or evoke other emotions?

4. Do I tend to judge or criticize others when they make mistakes or face challenges, or do I offer understanding and empathy?

5. When was the last time I helped someone, and what motivated me to do so?

6. How do I treat people who are different from me regarding background, beliefs, or culture?

7. Am I kind to myself? How do I react to my own mistakes and shortcomings?

8. Do I actively listen to others when they share their thoughts and feelings, or do I tend to dominate conversations?

9. How do I respond to acts of kindness directed toward me? Am I appreciative and grateful?

10. Do I hold grudges or forgive easily when someone wrongs me?

11. How do I handle conflicts and disagreements with others? Do I strive for understanding and resolution or become defensive or aggressive?

12. Do I engage in gossip or speak negatively about others?

13. How do I treat people in positions of service or lower social status?

14. Am I willing to step outside my comfort zone to help others, even if it inconveniences me?

15. How do I respond to people with different opinions or perspectives?

Improving Skills and Abilities Related to Kindness

Here are some skills and abilities that can help you cultivate more kindness:

- **Develop your capacity for empathy:** The ability to understand and share the feelings and perspectives of others is crucial for kindness. Practice putting yourself in someone else's shoes and truly listening to their experiences and emotions.
- **Become a good listener:** Practice active listening by giving full attention to others, maintaining eye contact, and offering verbal and non-verbal cues to show your engagement in the conversation.
- **Learn to regulate your emotions:** Being kind requires managing your emotions effectively. Learn techniques for calming yourself in stressful and social situations.
- **Be kind to yourself:** Cultivate self-compassion by treating yourself with the same care and understanding you would offer to a friend in need.
- **Practice mindfulness:** Becoming more present and attentive can make you more aware of your needs and those of others. Mindfulness allows you to observe your thoughts and emotions without judgment, which can lead to more compassionate responses toward yourself and everyone else.
- **Improve communication skills:** Effective communication is essential for expressing kindness. Improve verbal and non-verbal communication skills to convey warmth, empathy, and respect.
- **Learn to appreciate different perspectives:** Try to understand different viewpoints and consider the

feelings and needs of others when making decisions or offering help.

- **Practice gratitude:** Being grateful can help you appreciate the kindness of others and develop a positive outlook. Being thankful for the kindness you receive can inspire you to pay it forward.
- **Develop conflict resolution skills:** Learning constructive ways to resolve conflicts can prevent unkind behaviors and promote understanding and cooperation.
- **Learn about social awareness:** Develop your ability to read social cues and understand the emotions of others. Being socially aware can help you respond with kindness in various social situations.
- **Learn to be patient:** Kindness often requires patience, especially when dealing with challenging situations or difficult people.
- **Be generous:** Offer your time, resources, or support to others in need. Generosity strengthens the capacity for kindness.
- **Practice kindness:** Include kindness in your everyday interactions and seek out opportunities to help others. Develop a habit of frequently offering acts of kindness.

Books on Kindness

The following books explain the many ways we can be kind. They also share inspirational stories and research findings about kindness's role in giving and receiving support.

The Kindness Cure: How the Science of Compassion Can Heal Your Heart and Your World. Tara Cousineau draws on scientific research to show how kindness and compassion can lead to a healthier, happier life and foster positive connections with others.

The Power of Kindness: The Unexpected Benefits of Leading a Compassionate Life. Piero Ferrucci delves into the various aspects of kindness, showing how it benefits individuals and society, and he provides practical tips for cultivating kindness in everyday life.

The Five Side Effects of Kindness: This Book Will Make You Feel Better, Be Happier & Live Longer. David Hamilton explores the scientific evidence that kindness positively affects physical and mental well-being.

The Hidden Power of Kindness: A Practical Handbook for Souls Who Dare to Transform the World, One Deed at a Time. Lawrence Lovasik discusses the significance of small acts of kindness and their potential to create a more compassionate world.

Proactive Mental Health Building Block
Adaptability

Life brings many challenges and opportunities. Over time, work, relationships, and aging force us to adjust. Technological innovations, environmental degradation, and economic disruptions also call us to adapt. Everyday opportunities and disappointments come with our daily commute, grocery shopping, caring for family members, and tending to other responsibilities. To be alive means to have to adapt.

Adaptability refers to the capability to adjust to changes, new situations, or unforeseen challenges constructively and effectively. Adaptability has become crucial to surviving and thriving in a rapidly changing world. Fortunately, humans have a fantastic capacity to adapt to changing circumstances. As we shall see in the following chapters, several important skills and abilities enhance our capacity to be resilient and maintain well-being amidst challenges. Among these are being able to:

- Manage disappointment.
- Persist in the face of challenges.
- Be open to new ways of doing things.
- Consider your strengths before taking on tasks and challenges.
- Avoid seeing problems or bad news as permanent, pervasive (affecting all things), or personal (about you).

Adaptability is important to proactive mental health. Our capacity to handle change is a significant determinant of our experiences with other proactive mental health dimensions such as social connections, safety, purpose, and health behavior. Adaptability offers a protective cushion against life's uncertainties and challenges, promoting a healthier mental state and better overall well-being. Ideally, we would enhance our adaptability by surrounding ourselves with supportive cultural environments at work, at home, and in our communities, where people tend to have a sense of community, a shared vision, and a positive outlook.

How Culture Supports or Undermines Adaptability

Cultural support is important when we seek to become adaptable. Some cultures are rigid and reactive. In such workgroups, households, and communities, negativity and resentment can undermine the ability to adapt. Other cultures are more open to change. In such adaptable cultures, there tends to be:

- **A sense of community:** People get to know one another, trust one another, and care for one another during times of need.
- **A positive outlook:** People celebrate accomplishments, know their strengths, and are enthusiastic. A "can do" attitude is embraced, not ridiculed as unrealistic.
- **A shared vision:** People feel they are working cooperatively, with the same values, on matters of importance.

Chapter 13

Manage Disappointment

"Life is all about setbacks. But you have to face them, deal with them, and overcome them; so that you can get to the good stuff."

– DEREK JETER

"When one door of happiness closes, another opens; but often we look so long at the closed door that we do not see the one which has been opened for us."

- HELEN KELLER

LIFE SOMETIMES GOES less smoothly than planned. Sometimes, high hopes run up against complications and setbacks. Disappointment is a common and natural emotion that arises when our expectations or desires are unmet. Developing effective coping strategies to manage disappointment is crucial for maintaining psychological well-being.

Benefits of Being Able to Manage Disappointment

Successfully managing disappointment can provide several mental health benefits, such as:

- **Reduced stress and anxiety:** When people can effectively manage disappointment, they are less likely to experience excessive stress and anxiety in response to setbacks. They develop coping strategies that help regulate emotions and prevent them from becoming overwhelming, contributing to a more balanced and calm state of mind.

- **Improved self-confidence:** Successfully managing disappointment fosters a sense of self-efficacy and self-confidence. It reinforces the belief that you can cope with adversity and setbacks. This increased self-confidence positively affects various areas of life and improves mental health outcomes.

- **Improved mood:** Managing disappointment facilitates emotional regulation and prevents the development of persistent negative emotional states. Effectively managing disappointment makes people equipped to process and express their emotions, creating a greater sense of emotional balance and contentment.

- **Increased positive coping strategies:** Learning to handle disappointment encourages the development of positive coping strategies, such as pursuing self-care, seeking social support, engaging in problem-solving, and reframing negative thoughts. These coping strategies help manage disappointment and can be applied to other stressors and challenges in life, promoting overall mental health.

- **Improved relationship dynamics:** Effective disappointment management positively impacts interpersonal relationships. People who can constructively navigate disappointment are better equipped to communicate their needs, manage conflicts, and maintain healthier relationships.

- **Increased adaptability and growth mindset:** Handling disappointment cultivates an attitude of adaptability and a growth mindset. People become more open to learning from disappointments, exploring alternative solutions, and adjusting their goals when necessary. This mindset promotes personal growth, resilience, and a sense of optimism about future challenges.

Myths and Misunderstandings about Handling Disappointment

There are numerous myths and misunderstandings about how handling disappointment works, including:

Myth: "Managing disappointment means not feeling any negative emotions."

Reality: When facing disappointment, it is normal to experience negative emotions such as sadness, frustration, or anger. Handling disappointment does not imply suppressing or denying these emotions but rather acknowledging and processing them in a healthy way.

Myth: "Effective disappointment management means being immune to disappointment."

Reality: No one is immune to disappointment. Even people who possess strong coping skills experience disappointment at times. Handling disappointment is not about avoiding it altogether but developing strategies to manage and bounce back constructively.

Myth: "Handling disappointment means always staying positive."

Reality: Although maintaining a positive outlook can be beneficial, effective disappointment management does not require constant positivity. It is important to allow yourself to experience and process negative emotions. Constructive handling of disappointment involves a balanced perspective that acknowledges the situation's positive and negative aspects.

Myth: "Managing disappointment means never setting high expectations."

Reality: Setting high expectations can motivate and drive personal growth. However, having realistic expectations and preparing for possible setbacks or unmet goals is also important. Effective disappointment management involves a balance between setting challenging goals and being open to alternative outcomes.

Myth: "Managing disappointment is a sign of weakness or failure."

Reality: Handling disappointment effectively is not a reflection of weakness or failure but rather a demonstration of resilience, adaptability, and the willingness to learn and grow from the experience.

Myth: "Handling disappointment means immediately bouncing back and moving on."

Reality: Everyone processes and recovers from disappointment at their own pace. Managing disappointment involves giving oneself the time and space to heal, reflect, and learn from the experience. It is a gradual process that may include ups and downs.

Self-Assessment for Handling Disappointment

The following questions can help you determine your current ability to manage disappointment.

1. How do I typically react when faced with disappointment? Do I tend to become overwhelmed by negative emotions, or can I maintain a sense of balance and perspective?

2. Do I find it challenging to let go of disappointment and move forward, or can I adapt and adjust my expectations or goals when faced with setbacks?

3. What strategies do I typically use to navigate through disappointment? Are these strategies helpful in managing my emotions and promoting resilience?

4. Do I tend to blame myself excessively or engage in negative self-talk when experiencing disappointment, or can I show self-compassion and maintain a realistic perspective?

5. How do I view disappointments in the long run? Do I see them as temporary setbacks that can be learning opportunities, or do I tend to view them as permanent failures?

6. How does disappointment impact my overall well-being? Do I notice a significant negative impact on my mood, motivation, or self-esteem when faced with disappointments?

7. Do I seek support from others when dealing with disappointment, or do I tend to isolate myself? How does social support contribute to my ability to handle disappointment?

8. Have I noticed any patterns or recurring themes in my experiences with disappointment? Are there specific triggers or situations that challenge my ability to handle disappointment effectively?

9. What have I learned from past experiences with disappointment? How have I grown or adapted as a result of these experiences?

10. Do I have a growth mindset when it comes to disappointment? Am I open to learning from setbacks and exploring alternative solutions, or do I tend to get stuck in a negative mindset?

Improving Skills and Abilities for Managing Disappointment

There are a variety of skills and abilities that influence how well you manage disappointment, such as:

- **Normalizing Disappointment:** Recognize that experiencing disappointment is normal in life. Everyone encounters setbacks, unmet expectations, or failures at some point. Understanding that disappointment is a universal experience can help you realize you are not alone in feeling this way.

- **Goal Adjustment and Reframing:** Disappointment often stems from unmet goals or aspirations. In such cases, reassessing and adjusting those goals can be helpful. Often, disappointment arises when our expectations are unrealistic or overly rigid. Learning to set realistic expectations based on accurate information and considering alternative outcomes can help minimize disappointment. Flexibility in expectations allows for greater adaptability and resilience in the face of adversity. Identifying alternative paths or setting new, realistic goals can foster a sense of hope and motivation.

- **Cognitive Restructuring:** Disappointment is closely linked to our thoughts and interpretations of events. Cognitive restructuring involves challenging negative or unhelpful thought patterns and replacing them with more balanced and constructive thinking. This process helps reframe disappointments, allowing you to view them as opportunities for growth and learning.

- **Emotional Regulation:** Disappointment can trigger various emotions, including sadness, frustration, or anger. Emotional regulation skills are essential for managing these feelings. Techniques such as deep breathing, mindfulness, and engaging in activities that promote relaxation can help regulate emotions and prevent them from becoming overwhelming.

- **Self-Compassion:** Self-compassion involves treating oneself with understanding and acceptance. While it is important to recognize opportunities for self-improvement, refrain from being overly self-critical.
- **Seeking Social Support:** Sharing feelings of disappointment with trusted friends, family members, or professionals can provide emotional support and perspective. Talking about your experience can help you process your emotions and may lead to new insights.
- **Learning from Disappointment:** Disappointment can be a valuable learning opportunity. Reflecting on the experience, identifying lessons learned, and considering alternative strategies or approaches can promote personal growth and resilience. It can also help build problem-solving skills and develop effective strategies to prevent or navigate similar disappointments in the future.

Books on Managing Disappointment

The following books explore strategies for effectively managing disappointment.

Rising Strong: How the Ability to Reset Transforms the Way We Live, Love, Parent, and Lead. Brené Brown explores the process of bouncing back from disappointment and failure and the power of vulnerability in navigating challenging emotions.

The Gifts of Imperfection: Let Go of Who You Think You're Supposed to Be and Embrace Who You Are. Brené

Brown explores the power of vulnerability and embracing imperfections to deal with disappointment and cultivate a sense of self-worth.

When Things Fall Apart: Heart Advice for Difficult Times. Pema Chödrön, a Buddhist nun, offers wisdom and guidance on handling disappointment, loss, and uncertainty with compassion and courage.

Emotional Agility: Get Unstuck, Embrace Change, and Thrive in Work and Life. Susan David provides practical advice on handling emotions, including disappointment, and developing emotional resilience.

The Obstacle Is the Way: The Timeless Art of Turning Trials into Triumph. Ryan Holiday draws inspiration from Stoic philosophy and presents a framework for handling obstacles and transforming difficulties into opportunities for growth and success.

Chapter 14

Persist

"The road to success is dotted with many tempting parking spaces."

\- WILL ROGERS

"It's not that I'm so smart; it's just that I stay with problems longer."

\- ALBERT EINSTEIN

PERSISTENCE REFERS TO maintaining effort and determination when faced with obstacles, setbacks, or challenges. It involves continuing to work towards a goal or desired outcome despite difficulties.

Being able to persist is both a sign of mental health and a strategy for maintaining mental health. It isn't easy to persist when we are dispirited or distracted. Sticking with challenging goals focuses our thinking. The sense of accomplishment associated with achieving challenging goals can lift our spirits.

Persistence is not synonymous with stubbornness or refusing to change course. Sticking with unhealthy, hurtful, or unproductive goals impedes progress. Persistence involves the ability to adapt and adjust strategies when necessary. Sometimes, persistence involves recognizing when a particular goal is no longer feasible or pursuing an alternative path.

Persistence is not just an individual quality--our cultural environments can influence our ability to persist. In some cultures, it is a norm to abandon goals quickly; immediate goal achievement and gratification are expected, and goals that require patience and creativity rarely get achieved. In other cultures, sticking with a goal is highly prized. In such cultures, people are encouraged to persist, tackling challenging goals that require continued effort.

The Benefits of Persistence

There are several mental health benefits associated with persistence:

- **Sense of Mastery and Self-Efficacy:** Persistence can contribute to the belief in one's ability to accomplish tasks and overcome obstacles. Achieving goals through persistent efforts enhances self-confidence and self-esteem.
- **Reduced Stress and Anxiety:** Persistence allows individuals to tackle tasks and challenges proactively,

which can help reduce stress and anxiety levels. When individuals take consistent action toward their goals, they can feel more in control of their lives and experience greater calm and confidence.

- **Enhanced Coping Skills:** People who exhibit persistence tend to develop effective coping mechanisms and problem-solving skills. They are more likely to seek solutions, learn from setbacks, and adopt adaptive strategies. These skills can help manage stress, regulate emotions, and navigate difficult situations.

- **Increased Sense of Purpose and Meaning:** Individuals who persist in pursuing their goals may feel a greater sense of purpose. This sense of purpose can contribute to a more positive outlook, increased life satisfaction, and a reduced risk of developing mental health problems.

- **Improved Mood:** Persisting despite challenges fosters a positive emotional state. It helps promote feelings of accomplishment, satisfaction, and pride. People who demonstrate persistence are more likely to experience positive emotions such as joy, enthusiasm, and motivation, contributing to overall emotional well-being.

- **Positive Feedback Loop:** Persistence often leads to positive outcomes, reinforcing peoples' belief in their abilities and the value of their efforts. This positive feedback loop contributes to a greater sense of well-being as people see the direct impact of their persistence on their lives.

Myths and Misunderstandings about Persistence

There are several common myths and misunderstandings about persistence:

Myth: Persistence guarantees success.

Reality: Although persistence increases the likelihood of achieving goals, it does not guarantee success. Factors beyond an individual's control, such as external circumstances or limitations, can influence outcomes. Persistence increases the chances of success, but it is not a foolproof formula.

Myth: Being persistent means working harder and longer.

Reality: Persistence is not solely about working harder or longer but also maintaining consistent effort and determination. It involves managing resources effectively, including knowing when to take breaks, seek support, and prioritize self-care. Sustainable persistence requires a balanced approach that includes both focused effort and self-care.

Myth: Persistent people never experience doubt or setbacks.

Reality: Persistent individuals experience doubt and setbacks like anyone else. The key is their ability to navigate and learn from these challenges. Persistence involves resilience, learning from failures, and adapting strategies based on feedback and experience. Setbacks are viewed as learning opportunities rather than reasons to give up.

Myth: Persistence is an innate trait you have or don't have.

Reality: While some individuals may naturally exhibit higher levels of persistence, it is not solely an innate trait. Persistence can be developed through practice, mindset adjustments, and cultivating related skills such as goal setting, self-regulation, and resilience.

Myth: Persistent individuals are always serious and don't take breaks.

Reality: Persistent individuals understand the importance of balance. Taking breaks, engaging in leisure activities, and practicing self-care are vital for long-term persistence. Rest and rejuvenation are essential for sustaining motivation.

Persistence Self-Assessment

The following questions will help you determine your current ability to persist:

1. How do you respond to setbacks or obstacles when pursuing a goal? Do you tend to give up easily, or do you search for alternative solutions?
2. Think about a challenging task or goal you have pursued. How consistently did you work towards it over time? Did you maintain effort and motivation even when progress slowed, or obstacles arose?
3. How do you handle failure or mistakes? Do you view them as learning opportunities and adjust your strategies, or do they discourage you and hinder your persistence?

4. Reflect on your long-term goals. How well do you maintain focus and consistently work towards those goals? Can you break them down into smaller, manageable steps and persistently tackle each step?

5. Consider your response to external feedback or criticism. Are you open to feedback and willing to make necessary adjustments, or do you become defensive and resistant to change?

6. How do you balance persistence with self-care and rest? Do you recognize the importance of taking breaks and recharging, or do you push yourself relentlessly without considering your well-being?

7. Consider instances where you have successfully achieved challenging goals. What personal qualities or strategies helped you persist and ultimately succeed?

8. How do you manage your time and prioritize tasks? Can you allocate your resources effectively and consistently work towards your goals, or do you struggle with time management and task prioritization?

Strengthening Your Ability to Persist

Strengthening your ability to persist through challenges is a valuable skill that can lead to personal growth and success in various areas of life. Here are some strategies to help you build and enhance your persistence:

- **Set Clear Goals:** Establish clear and specific goals for yourself. Knowing what you want to achieve provides motivation and direction, making it easier to stay committed when obstacles emerge.

- **Break Tasks into Smaller Steps:** Divide larger tasks into smaller, manageable steps. This approach makes the process less overwhelming and allows you to celebrate progress along the way.
- **Develop a Growth Mindset:** Embrace a growth mindset, viewing challenges as opportunities for learning and growth rather than roadblocks. Believe that you can improve and develop your skills over time.
- **Maintain Focus:** Stay focused on your goals and avoid getting distracted by irrelevant or negative influences. Practice mindfulness and concentration techniques to enhance your ability to stay on track.
- **Apply Creative Solutions:** Some goals are achievable when reframed or looked at from a fresh perspective. Allow for creativity and be open to new approaches.
- **Embrace Perseverance:** Make a conscious effort to keep going even when things get tough. Recognize that persistence is a key factor in achieving long-term success.
- **Find Support:** Surround yourself with supportive and encouraging people who can motivate you during challenging times. Seek advice and feedback from mentors or coaches.
- **Celebrate Small Wins:** Acknowledge and celebrate your achievements, no matter how small they may seem. Recognizing progress can boost your motivation to keep going.

- **Learn from Role Models:** Study the stories of people who have succeeded through persistence and learn from their experiences. Knowing that others have overcome obstacles can be inspiring and informative.
- **Manage Emotional Reactions:** Strengthen your ability to manage stress, frustration, and disappointment effectively. Understand and regulate your emotions to maintain focus and motivation.
- **Take Care of Yourself:** Ensure you are physically and mentally well by getting enough rest, exercise, and relaxation. A healthy body and mind are better equipped to handle challenges.
- **Track Your Progress:** Keep a record of your efforts and achievements. Seeing your growth over time can motivate you to persist.
- **Adapt and Be Flexible:** Be open to adjusting your approach or changing course when necessary. Flexibility allows you to adapt to changing circumstances without losing sight of your goals.

Books about Persistence

Several books explore the themes of persistence and resilience in the face of challenges.

Rising Strong: How the Ability to Reset Transforms the Way We Live, Love, Parent, and Lead. Brené Brown explores getting back up after a fall, embracing vulnerability, and using these experiences to build resilience and persistence.

Grit: The Power of Passion and Perseverance. Angela Duckworth explores the concept of grit, a combination of passion and perseverance, and how it is a crucial factor in achieving success in various aspects of life.

Mindset: The New Psychology of Success. Carol Dweck introduces the concept of a growth mindset versus a fixed mindset and how adopting a growth mindset can foster persistence and achievement.

The Dip: A Little Book That Teaches You When to Quit (and When to Stick). Seth Godin explains how persistence can lead to success in the right situations but also emphasizes the importance of knowing when to quit unproductive endeavors.

The Compound Effect. Darren Hardy explains how small, consistent actions can lead to significant results over time, emphasizing the power of persistence in achieving success.

The Obstacle Is the Way: The Timeless Art of Turning Trials into Triumph. Ryan Holiday draws from Stoic philosophy and explores how facing obstacles and persevering through difficulties can lead to personal growth and success.

Keep Going: 10 Ways to Stay Creative in Good Times and Bad. Austin Kleon offers inspiration and practical advice on persisting in creative pursuits, even when facing challenges or feeling stuck.

The Last Lecture. Randy Pausch, a computer science professor diagnosed with terminal cancer, offers profound insights into living a meaningful life and persisting through challenges.

The Power of Positive Thinking. Norman Vincent Peale explores the role of positive thinking and persistence in overcoming obstacles and achieving personal and professional goals.

Perseverance. Margaret Wheatley discusses the concept of perseverance and its significance in our lives, communities, and organizations.

The Magic of Thinking Big. David Schwartz emphasizes the importance of thinking big, setting ambitious goals, and persisting in achieving them.

Chapter 15

Try New Things

"If you want something you've never had, you must be willing to do something you've never done."

- THOMAS JEFFERSON

"Do one thing every day that scares you."

- ELEANOR ROOSEVELT

BEING WILLING TO try new things means having an open and receptive attitude toward exploring unfamiliar experiences, ideas, or approaches. It involves proactively seeking healthy and relatively safe opportunities to step outside your comfort zone and embrace novelty. When you are willing to try new things, you exhibit the following characteristics:

- **Open-mindedness:** You are open to new perspectives, ideas, and possibilities. You are receptive to the thoughts and suggestions of others and are willing to consider alternative viewpoints.

- **Curiosity:** You have a sense of wonder and a desire to learn and discover. You seek new information and experiences to broaden your understanding of the world.
- **Flexibility:** You can adjust your mindset and actions to accommodate new situations or challenges. You are not rigid in your thinking or habits.
- **Courage:** Trying new things often involves facing the unknown and uncertainty. Being willing to try new things requires courage and a willingness to take calculated risks. You are ready to persevere and learn from setbacks or failures.
- **Resilience:** You understand that not everything may go as planned when trying something new.
- **Creativity:** Trying new things often requires creative thinking and problem-solving. You are willing to think outside the box and explore innovative solutions.
- **Initiative:** You actively seek new experiences or opportunities rather than waiting for them to come to you. You take the initiative to explore and try new things.
- **Positive attitude:** Being willing to try new things is often accompanied by an optimistic outlook. You approach new experiences with enthusiasm and a hopeful mindset.

American culture supports self-improvement and innovation. The economic system, science, and the arts embrace this bedrock value. Personal and professional success often comes with such courageous innovation. Trying new ways of doing things is a key component of creativity and innovation. By stepping outside established routines and exploring alternative approaches, people can generate novel ideas and solutions to problems.

Trying new ways of doing things promotes cognitive plasticity, which refers to the brain's ability to reorganize and form new neural connections. Individuals can enhance their cognitive flexibility and improve their ability to learn and adapt by engaging in novel tasks or problem-solving methods.

The Benefits of Being Willing to Try New Things

There are several important benefits associated with being open to trying new things:

- **Increased Resilience:** Trying new ways of doing things can contribute to greater resilience, which is the ability to bounce back from adversity and cope with life's challenges. By exploring alternative methods, people can develop adaptive skills and problem-solving strategies that enhance their ability to navigate difficult situations. This increased resilience can lead to improved mental well-being and a sense of personal mastery.

- **Enhanced Cognitive Functioning:** Engaging in novel activities or learning new skills stimulates cognitive processes such as attention, memory, and executive functioning. Trying new ways of doing things challenges the brain, promoting neuroplasticity and the formation of new neural connections. This can result in improved cognitive flexibility, creativity, and mental agility.

- **Reduced Anxiety and Stress:** Trying new ways of doing things can help break the cycle of routine and monotony that can contribute to stress and anxiety. Novelty and exploration stimulate the brain's reward systems and release dopamine, which can counteract the adverse effects of chronic stress. Additionally, by approaching challenges with a more open mindset, you may experience excitement and curiosity, reducing anxiety and promoting a more positive emotional state.

- **Increased Self-Confidence and Self-Efficacy:** Successfully trying new ways of doing things can boost self-confidence and self-efficacy—the belief in one's ability to accomplish tasks and achieve goals. By stepping out of your comfort zone and experiencing success in new endeavors, you gain a sense of personal competence and belief in your capabilities. This enhanced self-confidence can positively impact overall mental well-being and motivation.

- **Personal Growth and Self-Discovery:** Exploring new ways of doing things encourages personal growth and self-discovery. It allows you to challenge assumptions, expand perspectives, and discover hidden strengths and talents. This can foster a sense of meaning and fulfillment.

Myths and Misunderstandings about Being Open to Trying New Things

There are several common myths and misunderstandings about being open to trying new things:

Myth: Trying new things is only relevant to creative fields.

Reality: Although creativity is often associated with fields such as design and the arts, the ability to explore alternative methods is beneficial across various domains. It can enhance problem-solving skills, adaptability, and innovation in business, science, education, and personal development.

Myth: Trying new things always leads to success.

Reality: Although trying new approaches can lead to positive outcomes, it is important to recognize that not all attempts will be successful. Experimentation inherently involves a level of risk and uncertainty. Through failures and setbacks, people can learn valuable lessons and refine their strategies for future endeavors.

Myth: The ability to try new things is a fixed trait.

Reality: The inclination to try new things can be influenced by various factors, including individual beliefs, prior experiences, culture, and circumstances. Most importantly, the ability to try new things can be developed over time. With effort and practice, people can cultivate a more open mindset and a willingness to explore.

Myth: Trying new things is synonymous with impulsivity or lack of planning.

Reality: Trying new things does not imply haphazard or impulsive decision-making. It is about being open to new possibilities and considering alternative strategies thoughtfully and deliberately. Exploring new methods can be accompanied by careful evaluation, planning, and analysis to maximize safety and the chances of success.

Myth: Experts or people with a lot of experience don't need to try new things.

Reality: Everyone can benefit from trying new things. Sticking rigidly to established routines may limit growth and innovation. By challenging assumptions and exploring different approaches, experts can continue to expand their knowledge, refine their skills, and adapt to evolving circumstances.

Myth: Trying new ways of doing things requires radical changes.

Reality: Trying new approaches does not always necessitate a complete overhaul or drastic shift. It can involve small modifications, incremental improvements, or combining existing methods in novel ways. Even minor adjustments to established practices can lead to valuable insights and enhanced effectiveness.

Self-Assessment to Openness to Trying New Things

The following questions will help you determine your current ability to be open to pursuing new ways of doing things:

1. How comfortable am I with change and stepping out of my comfort zone?
2. Do I actively seek new experiences, ideas, or perspectives?
3. Am I willing to challenge my existing beliefs and assumptions?
4. How adaptable am I when faced with unexpected situations or obstacles?
5. Do I find myself stuck in routines and resistant to change?
6. How often do I try different strategies or methods when facing challenges?
7. Am I receptive to feedback and open to considering alternative perspectives?
8. How willing am I to take risks and embrace uncertainty?
9. Do I view failure as an opportunity for learning and growth?
10. Am I curious and interested in exploring new knowledge or skills?

Strengthening Your Ability to Be Open to Trying New Things

Here are some ways to help you embrace novelty and be more open to trying new things:

- **Be curious:** Ask questions. Be interested in exploring different perspectives and learning from others.
- **Learn new skills:** Continuously invest in learning and acquiring new skills. This will make it easier to adapt to new ways of doing things.

- **Challenge assumptions:** Question your existing beliefs and assumptions. Often, we hold ourselves back due to limiting beliefs.
- **Start small:** Begin with small changes and gradually work your way up. This can help you build confidence and momentum.
- **Take calculated risks:** Weigh the potential risks and rewards of trying something new. Sometimes, taking calculated risks can lead to exciting outcomes.
- **Seek inspiration:** Look for inspiration from books, documentaries, TED Talks, or successful people who have ventured into new territory.
- **Surround yourself with open-minded people:** Spend more time with people open to trying new things. Positive influences can motivate you to take similar steps.
- **Set clear goals:** Define your objectives and break them down into manageable steps. Having a clear purpose and a plan can provide direction and motivation.
- **Visualize success:** Imagine yourself succeeding in trying new things. Visualization can boost confidence and help you mentally prepare for new challenges.
- **Celebrate progress:** Acknowledge your efforts and progress, even if the outcome isn't perfect. Celebrating milestones will reinforce your motivation.
- **Be open to feedback:** Accept constructive feedback from others and use it to improve your approach.
- **Learn from failure:** See failures as learning experiences rather than setbacks. Analyze what went wrong, adapt, and try again.

- **Learn stress management and mindfulness techniques:** Being present and aware of your thoughts and emotions can help you overcome the fear and anxiety of trying new things.

Books about Being Open to Trying New Things

These books are about being open to trying new things.

Originals: How Non-Conformists Move the World. Adam Grant explores the habits and approaches of original thinkers and innovators. He discusses how these people challenge the status quo and develop new ideas, encouraging readers to embrace their originality and take risks.

Daring Greatly: How the Courage to Be Vulnerable Transforms the Way We Live, Love, Parent, and Lead. Brené Brown examines vulnerability and the courage to try new things and enter the unknown. The book discusses how vulnerability can lead to personal growth and more meaningful connections.

Designing Your Life: How to Build a Well-Lived, Joyful Life. Bill Burnett and Dave Evans offer practical tools and strategies to approach life as a design project, helping you try new approaches to create a fulfilling life.

Mindset: The New Psychology of Success. Carol Dweck explores the power of having a growth mindset, which encourages trying new things, embracing challenges, and seeing failures as opportunities to learn and improve.

Big Magic: Creative Living Beyond Fear. Elizabeth Gilbert encourages readers to pursue their creative passions and embrace curiosity. She advocates for exploring new artistic ventures without fear of judgment or failure.

Steal Like an Artist: 10 Things Nobody Told You About Being Creative. Austin Kleon encourages readers to embrace their creative side, take inspiration from others, and fearlessly explore new ideas.

Chapter 16

Consider Your Strengths

"Success is achieved by developing our strengths, not by eliminating our weaknesses."

- MARILYN VOS SAVANT

"Strengths are not just activities you're good at; they're activities that strengthen you. A strength is an activity that before you're doing it, you look forward to doing it; while you're doing it, time goes by quickly and you can concentrate; after you've done it, it seems to fulfill a need of yours."

- MARCUS BUCKINGHAM

SOMETIMES, IT IS possible to accomplish a task easily and without much thought. However, particularly challenging tasks require greater deliberation and skill development. To be successful, people must be aware of missing ingredients and how to acquire them. However, a singular focus on what's missing is likely to sap enthusiasm. Recognizing existing strengths and abilities is another important strategy for tackling challenging goals. Such a positive strengths-based mindset is also psychologically uplifting.

Considering your strengths before taking on challenges means analyzing your available resources, abilities, talents, and skills before facing a difficult situation, task, or goal. This can be broken down as follows:

- **Available Resources:** These are the tools or assets you have at your disposal. Resources can be tangible, like money, equipment, and technology, or intangible, like time, information, or social connections. To analyze your available resources, consider what you have access to that can help you overcome challenges or achieve goals.

- **Abilities:** These are the things you can do well. Abilities might be physical (such as strength or speed), cognitive (such as problem-solving or creative thinking), or emotional (such as empathy or resilience). To analyze your abilities, consider the tasks you excel at or where others often seek your help.

- **Talents:** These are natural aptitudes or skills. Unlike abilities, which can be learned or developed, talents are innate—you either have them or you don't. To analyze your talents, think about what comes naturally to you. Maybe you have a knack for music, art, athletics, mathematics, or anything else.

- **Skills:** These are specific things you've learned to do well, often through training or experience. Skills can be technical (like knowing how to code or repair a car) or soft (like communication skills or teamwork). To analyze your skills, consider what you've learned through education, training, or experience.

The Benefits of Considering Strengths First

Considering personal strengths before taking on tasks benefits performance and achievement and has significant positive implications for mental health and well-being. Among these benefits are:

- **Increased Confidence and Self-Efficacy:** When people recognize and leverage their strengths, it boosts their confidence and belief in their abilities. They develop a sense of self-efficacy, which is the belief that they can accomplish tasks. This increased confidence can reduce self-doubt, enhance resilience, and improve overall mental well-being.
- **Enhanced Motivation and Engagement:** Aligning tasks with strengths fosters intrinsic motivation and engagement. People feel a natural inclination and enthusiasm when they engage in activities that utilize their strengths. This heightened motivation promotes a state of flow, where they are fully immersed and absorbed in the task, leading to a sense of fulfillment and improved mental well-being.
- **Increased Positive Emotions and Well-Being:** Leveraging strengths is associated with increased positive

emotions such as joy, excitement, and satisfaction. Engaging in activities that align with strengths often leads to a sense of accomplishment, purpose, and fulfillment. These positive emotions contribute to well-being, resilience, and a positive outlook.

- **Reduced Stress and Burnout:** When people operate from a place of strength, they are more likely to experience a sense of competence and mastery in their tasks. This can reduce stress and prevent burnout because they are better equipped to handle challenges and demands. Leveraging strengths allows people to approach tasks with confidence and a sense of control, leading to improved mental health outcomes.
- **Improved Self-Acceptance and Authenticity:** Emphasizing strengths fosters self-acceptance and authenticity. People can embrace their unique qualities and abilities by recognizing and utilizing their strengths. This acceptance promotes self-esteem, self-worth, and a positive self-concept, leading to greater psychological well-being.
- **Resilience and Coping Skills:** When faced with setbacks or adversities, people who know their strengths can draw upon them as resources, enabling them to persevere and find effective solutions. This resilience contributes to better mental health outcomes and adaptive coping strategies.

Myths and Misunderstandings about Focusing on Strengths
Understanding and dispelling these myths is essential for harnessing the benefits of your strengths:

Myth: Focusing on strengths means ignoring weaknesses.

Reality: Emphasizing strengths does not imply neglecting weaknesses. Acknowledging areas for growth and improvement is crucial for personal development. However, recognizing and leveraging strengths provides a foundation for success, motivation, and enhanced performance. A strengths perspective uses strengths to address weaknesses.

Myth: Strengths are fixed and unchangeable traits.

Reality: Although strengths have a stable foundation, they are not rigid or fixed traits. Research suggests that strengths can be developed through intentional practice and learning. With effort and experience, people can refine their existing strengths and even acquire new ones.

Myth: Strengths are limited to specific domains or professions.

Reality: Strengths are not confined to specific areas of life or work. They are also personal attributes that can be applied across various domains and tasks. For example, someone with excellent communication skills can leverage this strength in different contexts, such as team collaboration, public speaking, customer service, and personal relationships.

Myth: All strengths are positive.

Reality: Just because you are good at something doesn't mean that strength is good for yourself or others. For example, the strength of being highly persuasive can mean that you fail to consider others' needs. You can modify your strengths to incorporate the needs of all parties better.

Myth: Focusing on strengths is self-centered or egotistical.

Reality: Emphasizing personal strengths is not synonymous with self-centeredness. Recognizing and utilizing strengths is a positive and constructive approach that benefits individuals and those around them. By leveraging their strengths, people can contribute to team success, help others, and make meaningful contributions to their communities.

Myth: Strengths-based approaches ignore challenges and adversity.

Reality: Strengths-based approaches do not discount challenges or adversity. Instead, they emphasize resilience and overcoming obstacles by utilizing personal strengths. By identifying and drawing upon strengths, people can navigate difficulties more effectively, find creative solutions, and maintain a positive mindset during challenging times.

Myth: Strengths-based approaches lead to complacency.

Reality: Leveraging strengths does not imply complacency or settling for mediocrity. On the contrary, it often fosters motivation, engagement, and a drive for excellence. When people operate from a place of strength, they are more likely to pursue continuous growth and seek opportunities for further development.

Self-Assessment for Recognizing Strengths

The following questions will help you determine your current ability to focus on strengths when pursuing goals:

1. How well do I know and understand my strengths?
2. Can I confidently articulate my top strengths and describe how they manifest in different contexts?
3. Do I clearly understand which tasks or activities align with my strengths?
4. Am I aware of any blind spots or areas where I may overlook or underutilize my strengths?
5. Do I actively seek out tasks or projects that align with my strengths?
6. How do I prioritize tasks that allow me to leverage my strengths versus those that don't?
7. Am I open to exploring new tasks that could further develop or complement my existing strengths?
8. Before starting a task, do I consider how I can apply my strengths to enhance performance and outcomes?
9. Do I identify potential challenges and strategize how to use my strengths to address them effectively?
10. Am I mindful of any potential limitations or areas where my strengths may not be as applicable?
11. How well do I adapt my strengths to different task requirements and contexts?
12. Can I identify alternative ways to utilize my strengths in situations that may not be directly applicable?
13. After completing a task, do I reflect on how effectively I leveraged my strengths?

14. Am I receptive to feedback and opportunities for growth related to my strengths?
15. How do I incorporate lessons learned from previous tasks into future planning and utilizing my strengths?
16. Do I notice positive changes in my motivation, engagement, and overall well-being when I consider and leverage my strengths?
17. Can I recognize tangible outcomes and achievements that result from utilizing my strengths?

Strengthening Your Ability to Recognize Your Strengths

Here are some strategies to help you focus on and enhance your strengths:

- **Self-Evaluation:** Reflect on your experiences and performance in different situations. Identify which skills and abilities you naturally excel at and enjoy using.
- **Feedback:** Ask colleagues, mentors, or others who understand your work about your strengths. These people can provide insights that you might not have realized yourself.
- **Strengths Assessment:** Use formal assessment tools, like the StrengthsFinder or VIA Survey, to help identify your key strengths.
- **Education and Training:** Once you've identified your strengths, look for ways to enhance them. This could involve taking classes, attending workshops, or pursuing certifications in your areas of strength.
- **Practice:** Regularly exercising your strengths can lead to improvement over time.

- **Mentorship and Coaching:** Seek mentorship or coaching from individuals who excel in the areas you want to strengthen. Their guidance and feedback can be instrumental in your development.
- **Stretch Projects:** Take on projects or roles that stretch your abilities and force you to rely on your strengths. This can both highlight and improve your capabilities.
- **Mindset:** Maintain a growth mindset, which is the belief that your abilities can be developed with effort and practice. This perspective encourages learning and personal development.
- **Physical Well-being:** Physical and mental health can significantly impact your abilities. Ensure you get proper nutrition, exercise, sleep, and stress management.

Books on a Strengths Orientation

The following books focus on how to mobilize personal strengths.

Now, Discover Your Strengths. Marcus Buckingham and Donald Clifton introduce the StrengthsFinder assessment and provide insights into how to focus on utilizing your strengths rather than fixing your weaknesses.

Go Put Your Strengths to Work: 6 Powerful Steps to Achieve Outstanding Performance. Marcus Buckingham offers actionable advice on identifying and harnessing your strengths at work.

The Power of Character Strengths: Appreciate and Ignite Your Positive Personality. Ryan Niemiec and Robert

McGrath use the VIA character strengths framework to help readers understand and apply their strengths.

Strengths-Based Leadership: Great Leaders, Teams, and Why People Follow. Tom Rath and Barry Conchie provide insights into using your strengths to become a more effective leader.

Chapter 17

Embrace Realistic Optimism

"The pessimist complains about the wind; the optimist expects it to change; the realist adjusts the sails."
        - WILLIAM ARTHUR WARD

"Optimism is a strategy for making a better future. Because unless you believe that the future can be better, you are unlikely to step up and take responsibility for making it so."
        - NOAM CHOMSKY

AN OPTIMISTIC PERSPECTIVE is a belief that events turn out for the best. Realistic optimism embraces a positive outlook and the possibility that a hoped-for result may not be likely or possible. Unrealistic optimism can lead to poor decision-making, as a person might ignore important information, neglect to prepare for challenges, or fail to take necessary precautions. Realistic optimism is grounded in the situation and still mobilizes the hope and enthusiasm required for success.

The Benefits of Realistic Optimism

Here are some of the mental health benefits associated with realistic optimism:

- **Lower Levels of Distress:** Realistic optimism helps lower stress and distress levels in challenging situations. It allows people to interpret these situations in a more positive light or believe they can cope with them effectively.
- **Reduced Risk of Depression:** An optimistic perspective is associated with a lower risk of developing symptoms of depression. This could be due to realistic optimists employing more adaptive coping strategies.
- **Higher Life Satisfaction:** People with optimistic thinking often report higher satisfaction with their lives than those with pessimistic perspectives.
- **Better Coping Skills:** People with optimistic thinking are more likely to employ positive coping strategies, such as problem-solving, seeking social support, or viewing challenges as opportunities for growth.
- **Greater Resilience:** Optimistic thinking can help people to bounce back from adversity more quickly and effectively. They often interpret setbacks as temporary and external rather than as lasting and inherent flaws in themselves.

- **Reduced Anxiety:** Some studies suggest that optimism might be linked to lower anxiety levels. Positive expectations about the future can counteract the worry and rumination that fuel anxiety.
- **Increased Mood:** Optimism positively correlates with subjective well-being, positive emotions, and a sense of purpose in life.
- **Boosted Immune Functioning:** People with optimistic thinking tend to have more robust immune responses. This can lead to physical and psychological benefits, as good physical health promotes mental well-being.
- **Better Stress Management:** People with optimistic thinking usually perceive stressors as less threatening, which can reduce the body's stress responses. This can help protect mental health in the long run.
- **More Healthy Behaviors:** People with optimistic thinking are often more proactive about their health, leading to behaviors that can have mental health benefits, like exercise, balanced nutrition, and regular medical check-ups.

Myths and Misunderstandings about Realistic Optimism

There are several myths and misconceptions surrounding realistic optimism, such as:

Myth: Optimism ignores reality.

Reality: One of the most prevalent myths is that optimists are naïve or in denial about reality. In truth, healthy optimism doesn't involve ignoring adverse facts but instead focusing on potential positive outcomes and solutions.

Myth: Optimism is inborn and can't be changed.

Reality: Genetics and upbringing can influence optimism, but it's also a learnable skill. Techniques like cognitive behavioral therapy and positive psychology interventions can help cultivate optimism.

Myth: Being optimistic means never feeling sad or anxious.

Reality: Everyone, regardless of their general outlook, experiences a range of emotions. Being optimistic doesn't mean you will never feel down or anxious; you will generally expect positive outcomes and can bounce back from challenges more effectively.

Myth: Being optimistic leads to complacency.

Reality: Some believe that if you're optimistic, you won't take action because you assume everything will turn out fine. However, people with optimistic thinking often feel more empowered to affect change because they believe their efforts can lead to positive outcomes.

Myth: Being optimistic means always being cheerful.

Reality: Having an optimistic outlook doesn't equate to being perpetually cheerful or bubbly. It's about expecting good outcomes in the future, not necessarily displaying a particular demeanor.

Myth: Pessimism is always bad.

Reality: In some situations, a more cautious or skeptical view can lead to better decision-making. The key is to balance the right amount of skepticism for the situation. For example, an airplane pilot or surgeon needs a certain amount of pessimism that motivates them to watch out for possible problems.

Myth: Being optimistic means not preparing for the worst.

Reality: A person who thinks optimistically might prepare just as thoroughly as someone expecting the worst but does so with the expectation of overcoming challenges.

Myth: Optimism guarantees success.

Reality: Although optimism can contribute to resilience, improved well-being, and better health outcomes, it doesn't guarantee success. It can, however, improve how you cope with challenges and setbacks.

Myth: Optimism is just "wishful thinking."

Reality: This myth assumes that optimism is passive—just hoping things will turn out well. In reality, many people who embrace optimism actively work towards their desired outcomes, fueled by their belief in possible success.

Myth: Optimism is the same as positive thinking.

Reality: Although they're related, they're not synonymous. Positive thinking is about pushing positive thoughts, while optimism is a broader expectation of good outcomes, even when acknowledging challenges.

Realistic Optimism Self-Assessment

The following questions will help you determine your current ability to adopt a mindset of realistic optimism:

1. Can I identify multiple causes for adverse events rather than placing the blame solely on one factor or person (including myself)?
2. When bad things happen, do I see the problem as affecting everything?
3. When bad things happen, do I tend to see them as temporary setbacks rather than permanent ones?
4. Do my expectations usually align with likely outcomes rather than what I hope or fear will happen?
5. Do I regularly weigh the pros and cons of a situation before I act?
6. Do I generally expect things to go well for me in the future?
7. Do I believe that more good things than bad will happen to me?
8. When I encounter a challenge, do I believe I can find a way to overcome it?
9. Do I believe that my actions can influence the outcome of events?
10. Am I hopeful about what the future holds for me?
11. Do I believe I can achieve my long-term goals, even if there might be obstacles along the way?
12. Do I believe that most people have good intentions?

13. When faced with challenges or failure, do I see it as a learning opportunity?
14. When I succeed, do I recognize and acknowledge my role in that success?
15. Do I seek solutions and ways to cope rather than ruminating on the problem?
16. Do I seek support or feedback when grappling with negative thoughts or challenging situations?
17. Am I open to others' perspectives, and do I use them to challenge my negative thought patterns?
18. Do I use coping strategies that are adaptive and constructive, such as problem-solving, seeking support, or reframing challenges?
19. When faced with obstacles, do I remind myself of past challenges I've overcome?

Strengthening Your Realistic Optimism

Here are some strategies to develop a realistic and optimistic mindset:

- **Gather Information:** Make judgments based on evidence, facts, and a clear understanding of circumstances. Regularly ask yourself if you're making assumptions without evidence.
- **Reframe Negative Thoughts:** Challenge and replace negative thoughts with more positive or neutral interpretations. For instance, instead of thinking, "I can't do this," try, "I will do the best I can."
- **Practice Gratitude:** Regularly note things you're grateful for. This can shift focus from what's lacking or negative to what's abundant and positive in your life.

- **Set Realistic Goals:** Break tasks into manageable steps and celebrate small victories. Achieving these smaller goals can boost confidence and reinforce an optimistic outlook.

- **Focus on Solutions:** Instead of dwelling on problems, redirect your energy towards finding solutions or positive coping strategies.

- **Practice Positive Affirmations:** Repeating positive and uplifting statements to yourself can help shift your mindset over time.

- **Visualize Positive Outcomes:** Spend time visualizing a successful version of an event or goal. This can train your mind to be more hopeful about future outcomes.

- **Read Uplifting Stories:** Seek out inspiring stories of individuals who've overcome challenges. This can provide motivation and a sense of possibility.

- **Limit Exposure to Negativity:** Be mindful of the negative news or media you consume. Try to balance it with positive content. Maximize your contact with positive and supportive people.

- **Stay Present:** Engage in mindfulness or meditation practices. Being present can reduce anxiety about the future and promote a more balanced perspective.

- **Seek Out the Silver Lining:** In difficult situations, ask yourself if there's anything you can learn or any potential positives from it.

- **Limit "Catastrophic Thinking":** Avoid focusing on the worst-case scenario when faced with setbacks. Instead, consider multiple outcomes, including positive ones.

- **Practice Resilience:** Recognize that setbacks are a part of life. Focus on building resilience to bounce back from challenges with a hopeful perspective.
- **Nurture Your Health:** Regular exercise, a balanced diet, and adequate sleep can boost mood and foster a more optimistic outlook. Physical health and mental well-being are closely intertwined.

Books about Optimism

Books on optimism span genres from self-help to scientific research.

The Antidote: Happiness for People Who Can't Stand Positive Thinking. Oliver Burkeman provides a counterintuitive take on happiness and positive thinking. This book challenges mainstream self-help advice and provides a fresh perspective on optimism.

Bright-sided: How Positive Thinking Is Undermining America. Barbara Ehrenreich provides a critical look at the culture of forced positivity. Ehrenreich challenges the sometimes-blind optimism promoted in modern society.

The Power of Positive Thinking. Norman Vincent Peale offers practical advice to maintain an optimistic attitude toward life's challenges.

Learned Optimism: How to Change Your Mind and Your Life. Martin Seligman, a pioneer in positive psychology, delves into the benefits of optimism and provides strategies to develop it.

The Optimism Bias: A Tour of the Irrationally Positive Brain. Tali Sharot offers a neuroscientist's perspective on why humans are hardwired for hope.

Proactive Mental Health Building Block
Purpose

A sense of purpose refers to the feeling that one's life has meaning, significance, and direction. A sense of purpose can be rooted in various aspects of life, including career, relationships, spirituality, hobbies, and societal contributions. Each person's sense of purpose can be unique and deeply personal. What resonates deeply with one person might not hold the same significance for another. A personal purpose often emerges from a blend of personal experiences, values, passions, and aspirations. Each of us can enjoy multiple purposes. Here are some examples of personal purposes that might resonate:

- **Learning and Growth:** Exploring new subjects and pursuing new understandings can be fulfilling.
- **Service to Others:** To serve others by helping those in need or less fortunate.
- **Teaching:** To educate and inspire the next generation to reach their full potential.
- **Creative Expression:** To express yourself through art, music, or writing and to inspire others to find their voice.
- **Spiritual Fulfillment:** To align with your spiritual beliefs and seek a more profound spiritual connection.
- **Family and Relationships:** To be the best parent, partner, or friend you can be, nurturing and supporting your loved ones and receiving their love and support.
- **Advocacy and Change:** To champion social justice causes and work towards creating a more equitable society.
- **Environmental Stewardship:** To protect and restore the environment for future generations.
- **Health and Wellness:** To lead a healthy lifestyle and inspire others to do the same.
- **Innovation:** To innovate, invent, or develop solutions to pressing problems.
- **Leadership:** To guide and support others, perhaps leading by example.

- **Adventure and Experience:** To explore the world, immerse yourself in different cultures, and understand diverse perspectives.
- **Craftsmanship:** To hone a craft or skill, whether it's woodworking, cooking, or any other discipline.
- **Legacy Building:** To leave a lasting impact or legacy, ensuring your actions and contributions benefit future generations.
- **Community Building:** To strengthen and uplift your community, creating connections and fostering a sense of belonging.

The following chapters highlight different aspects of purpose. The first examines how you can make a difference; when people have a sense of purpose, they often feel they are making a difference. The second chapter is about doing what is meaningful; people with a sense of purpose regularly do things that give their lives meaning. The third chapter is about identifying your passion and committing to actions that align with that passion. Together, these skills and abilities can strengthen your purpose.

Creating and maintaining a sense of purpose requires high levels of mental functioning. Much overlap exists between the proactive mental health dimension of purpose and other dimensions, such as presence, connection, and adaptability. Our purpose often involves social relationships, and maintaining purpose often requires an ability to adapt to changing circumstances. Purpose often requires reflection, being psychologically present, and observant.

A positive relationship exists between mental health and having a sense of purpose. Among these benefits are:

- **Well-being and Satisfaction:** People who report having a clear sense of purpose in life often have enhanced well-being and more life satisfaction than those who don't. A clear sense of purpose can offer direction, motivate actions, and influence behaviors, leading to more meaningful and fulfilling experiences.

- **Reduced Risk of Mental Health Disorders:** Some research suggests that a strong sense of purpose can protect against the development of certain mental health disorders. For example, people with a clear sense of purpose may be less likely to experience depression, anxiety, or other mood disorders.

- **Coping and Resilience:** A sense of purpose can bolster a person's ability to cope with stressors, setbacks, or traumas. It can provide a reason to persevere, enhance resilience, and offer a perspective to make challenges seem more surmountable.

- **Cognitive Functioning:** Some studies of older adults have found a positive relationship between having a sense of purpose and better cognition. A strong sense of purpose can be associated with a reduced risk of cognitive decline and Alzheimer's disease.

- **Improved Sleep:** A sense of purpose correlates with better sleep quality. This could be due to reduced levels of anxiety and rumination, which can interfere with sleep.

- **Substance Use and Abuse:** Having a clear purpose might reduce the risk of substance use and abuse. People with purpose may find healthier coping mechanisms and not rely on substances to fill a void or manage emotions.

How Culture Supports or Undermines Purpose

Cultures play an important role in supporting or undermining an individual's sense of purpose. For example, many people derive much of their purpose from work. When jobs are lost, careers stagnate, or the work is unproductive, the sense of purpose is diminished. Culture also plays an important role in determining people's ability to derive purpose from religious pursuits, artistic expression, or raising a family. Culture can support or undermine such purposes. Ideally, the culture would provide abundant opportunities and ongoing support for individuals to pursue their sense of purpose.

Chapter 18

Make a Difference

"Never believe that a few caring people can't change the world. For, indeed, that's all who ever have."
                                                    - MARGARET MEAD

"What you do makes a difference, and you have to decide what kind of difference you want to make."
                                                    - JANE GOODALL

MAKING A DIFFERENCE means positively influencing, changing, or contributing to a situation, individual, or group. Making a difference is a multifaceted and profoundly personal experience. It involves both acting and feeling that your efforts count. For some, making a difference might mean impacting thousands of lives or changing the course of history. For others, it could be as simple as improving one person's day.

Making a difference can entail:

- **Purpose and Meaning:** A sense of purpose is the heart of making a difference. You feel that your actions align with a deeper meaning or mission beyond mere daily routine or personal gain.

- **Impact and Change:** The tangible or intangible changes you make in the lives of others, the environment, or a situation can foster the feeling of making a difference. For instance, a teacher seeing a student's progress or an activist seeing a policy change might feel they are making a difference.

- **Legacy and Longevity:** The belief that your efforts will have lasting effects can also contribute to this feeling. For example, planting trees may be seen as positively impacting future generations.

- **Affirmation and Feedback:** Sometimes, direct feedback or appreciation from others can evoke the sensation of making a difference. A simple "thank you" or acknowledgment can be powerful.

- **Personal Growth:** Making a difference often aligns with personal development. As you contribute to causes or help others, you learn and grow, reinforcing the feeling of having a meaningful impact.

- **A Sense of Fulfillment:** A profound sense of satisfaction can come from knowing that your actions have positively impacted others or a cause.

- **Connection:** Making a difference often involves connecting deeply with others. This shared experience or collaborative effort towards a positive goal can instill a profound sense of community and belonging.

- **Moral and Ethical Alignment:** Feeling like you're making a difference might also arise from a sense that you are doing the "right" thing or acting according to your personal or societal values.

The Benefits of Feeling Like You Are Making a Difference

There are mental health benefits associated with feeling like you are making a difference:

- **Enhanced Self-Efficacy:** When you believe your actions can have a positive impact, it boosts your belief in your ability to accomplish goals and overcome challenges. Increased self-efficacy is associated with reduced levels of stress, anxiety, and depression, as well as improved coping skills and resilience.
- **Positive Emotions and Happiness:** Engaging in activities that make a difference often leads to the experience of positive emotions such as joy, gratitude, and fulfillment. These positive emotions contribute to happiness and life satisfaction.
- **Reduced Psychological Distress:** Feeling like you are making a difference can act as a buffer against psychological distress. When you have a sense of purpose and contribute to something meaningful, you are less likely to experience symptoms of anxiety, depression, and other mental health challenges.
- **Improved Social Connections:** Making a difference often involves engaging with others and contributing to the well-being of individuals or communities. This fosters social connections and a sense of belonging, which is crucial for mental health.

- **Increased Resilience and Coping Skills:** Feeling like you are making a difference can enhance resilience—the ability to bounce back from setbacks and cope with adversity. When you are engaged in meaningful activities, you develop a sense of purpose that provides motivation to navigate challenges.
- **Positive Impact on Self-Identity:** Making a difference aligns actions with personal values and beliefs, promoting a positive self-identity. Engaging in meaningful activities and contributing to others' well-being enhances self-perception, self-worth, and self-esteem.

Myths and Misunderstandings about Making a Difference

There are numerous myths or misunderstandings about feeling like you are making a difference:

Myth 1: Making a difference requires grand gestures or significant achievements.

Reality: Making a difference can come in various forms and does not necessarily require grand gestures or major accomplishments. Small acts of kindness, daily contributions to a cause, or positively impacting individuals can make a meaningful difference.

Myth 2: Feeling like you are making a difference solely depends on external validation or recognition.

Reality: Although external validation and recognition can enhance the feeling of making a difference, it is not the sole determinant. Internal validation, personal satisfaction, and alignment with one's values and goals play crucial roles in experiencing a sense of making a difference.

Myth 3: Making a difference is limited to specific professions or roles.

Reality: Making a difference is a mindset and can be practiced in any profession or sphere of life, such as personal relationships, community involvement, or even within oneself. Any action that positively impacts others or contributes to a greater good can create a sense of making a difference.

Myth 4: Making a difference is a one-time event or achievement.

Reality: Feeling like you are making a difference is an ongoing process. It is not limited to a single event or achievement. It involves sustained effort, consistent actions, and a long-term perspective. Making a difference often requires dedication and persistence over time.

Myth 5: Making a difference is about the outcome or visible impact.

Reality: Although outcomes and visible impact are important, making a difference is also significant. Engaging in activities aligned with one's values, personal growth, and learning from experiences are valuable aspects of feeling like you are making a difference. The journey and the intrinsic rewards from the process contribute to the overall sense of purpose and fulfillment.

Self-Assessment for Feeling You Are Making a Difference

Here are some questions you can ask yourself to determine your ability to feel like you are making a difference:

1. Am I contributing to causes or issues that are important to me?
2. Do my activities and actions align with my values and beliefs?
3. Do I prioritize and invest time and effort in areas that reflect my values?
4. How do my actions positively impact others' lives or well-being?
5. Can I create positive change or contribute to meaningful outcomes?
6. Do I see tangible results or improvements because of my efforts?
7. Do I feel a sense of purpose and meaning when I engage in activities related to making a difference?
8. Do I experience joy, pride, or accomplishment from the difference I believe I am making?
9. Have I received feedback or recognition from others regarding the impact of my actions?
10. Do I actively seek and value feedback from those directly or indirectly affected by my efforts?
11. How do others perceive the difference I am making, and does it align with my perception?
12. Can I maintain motivation and passion for making a difference over the long term?

13. Am I continually learning and growing through my efforts to make a difference?

Strengthening Your Ability to Make a Difference

Making a difference is a journey, not a destination. Every step you take to strengthen your ability will contribute to a more significant impact. Here are some strategies for increasing your capacity to make a difference:

- **Self-awareness:** Understand your strengths, passions, and values. The more you're aware of what drives you, the better positioned you are to use those strengths to make a difference.
- **Education and Training:** Seek knowledge and skills to amplify your efforts. Whether through formal education, workshops, or self-taught practices, always strive to learn more.
- **Set Clear Goals:** Determine what you want to achieve and break down large goals into smaller, actionable steps. This provides direction and milestones to measure your progress.
- **Network:** Connect with like-minded individuals, join organizations, or attend events that align with your mission. Collaborative efforts often amplify impact.
- **Stay Informed:** Be aware of current events and trends related to your area of interest. Understanding the bigger picture can help you make more informed decisions.
- **Volunteer:** Offer your time, skills, and expertise to causes or organizations that resonate with you. This

hands-on experience is invaluable and can provide a direct sense of making a difference.

- **Mentorship:** Seek mentors with experience in your area of interest and consider mentoring others. Sharing knowledge and experiences can create a ripple effect of positive change.

- **Practice Empathy and Active Listening:** To make a genuine difference, it's essential to understand the needs and perspectives of others. This can guide your actions in more impactful ways.

- **Adaptability:** Be willing to adjust your strategies if something isn't working. Stay open to feedback and be flexible in your approach.

- **Self-care:** Ensure you care for your mental, emotional, and physical health. Burnout can hinder your ability to make a difference. Recharge and refuel regularly.

- **Stay Resilient:** Making a difference often comes with challenges. Stay persistent and remember why you started. Celebrate small wins along the way.

- **Advocate:** Use your voice to raise awareness. This can be through writing, speaking engagements, social media, or simply talking to friends and family about the causes you care about.

- **Financial Support:** If you have the means, consider donating to causes or organizations that align with your values. Even small donations can contribute to making a difference.

- **Practice Everyday Kindness:** Remember that making a difference isn't only about grand gestures. Small acts of kindness, understanding, or assistance in daily life can be immensely impactful.

- **Reflect and Evaluate:** Review your goals, methods, and outcomes. This introspection can offer insights into what's working and where you might need to adjust your approach.

Books about Making a Difference

The psychological benefits of making a difference, often intertwined with concepts of purpose, altruism, and the intrinsic rewards of helping others, have been explored in various books, including:

Man's Search for Meaning. Viktor E. Frankl's classic work delves into Frankl's experiences in Nazi concentration camps and his development of logotherapy, a form of psychotherapy that emphasizes the search for meaning in life.

Give and Take: Why Helping Others Drives Our Success. Adam Grant, a professor at Wharton, presents the idea that success doesn't have to come at others' expense. This book explores the psychological and professional benefits of giving.

The Compassionate Instinct: The Science of Human Goodness. Edited by Dacher Keltner, Jason Marsh, and Jeremy Adam Smith, this collection of essays explores the evolutionary basis for altruism and the psychological benefits of compassion and making a difference.

Doing Good Better: How Effective Altruism Can Help You Make a Difference. William MacAskill focuses on the effectiveness of doing good. The book also delves into the positive psychological effects of knowing one's efforts are genuinely making an impact.

Altruism: The Power of Compassion to Change Yourself and the World. Matthieu Ricard combines research, anecdotes, and real-world examples to argue that altruism, the selfless concern for the well-being of others, can be cultivated and lead to a happier, more compassionate, and more resilient society.

The Paradox of Generosity: Giving We Receive, Grasping We Lose. Christian Smith and Hilary Davidson provide evidence from a study showing that those who give away more resources – money, time, and skills – often reap surprising advantages.

Chapter 19

Do What's Meaningful

"The two most important days in your life are the day you are born and the day you find out why."
— MARK TWAIN

"Meaning is not something you stumble across, like the answer to a riddle or the prize in a treasure hunt. Meaning is something you build into your life."
— JOHN GARDNER

DOING MEANINGFUL THINGS refers to engaging in actions, pursuits, or endeavors that resonate with one's values, beliefs, and purpose. These activities often provide a more profound sense of fulfillment, connection, and significance beyond mere momentary pleasure or short-term satisfaction. They align with an individual's core principles, contribute to their greater life purpose, or positively impact the broader community or world. Meaningful activities evoke a sense of purpose and contribute to lasting well-being and contentment.

Culture plays an important role in offering opportunities for meaningful action. People seek and find meaning in many ways, depending on their cultural environments, personal beliefs, values, interests, and circumstances. Ideally, cultural environments provide abundant opportunities to pursue personal meaning. Here are some ways in which people can pursue and experience meaning in their lives:

- **Relationships:** Building deep and genuine relationships with family, friends, and significant others can be sources of meaning.
- **Parenting and Caring for Children:** Raising children and being involved in their development can provide meaning for many.
- **Work and Careers:** Engaging in work that aligns with personal values or passions, whether it's through traditional employment, entrepreneurship, or volunteer efforts, can be a source of meaning.
- **Spirituality and Religion:** Meaning can be derived from following religious practices, engaging in spiritual rituals, or being part of a faith community.
- **Learning:** Continual personal growth through education, reading, workshops, or other avenues of gaining knowledge and skills can be a source of meaning.
- **Art and Creativity:** Many people find meaning through expressing themselves through writing, painting, music, dance, or other creative endeavors.

- **Philanthropy and Service:** Volunteering, supporting charitable causes, and helping those in need can be sources of meaning.
- **Activism:** People find meaning through advocating for social, political, or environmental causes and working towards positive change.
- **Nature and Environment:** Connecting with nature—whether through hiking, gardening, simply spending time outdoors, or contributing to conservation efforts—can provide a deep sense of meaning.
- **Health and Fitness:** Some people find meaning through pursuing physical wellness, whether it's through sports, exercise, or adopting a healthy lifestyle.
- **Travel and Cultural Exploration:** Learning about other cultures, histories, and ways of life can be a source of meaning.
- **Mentoring and Teaching:** Sharing knowledge and experiences with others and guiding them in personal or professional growth can be a source of meaning.
- **Craftsmanship:** Some people find meaning through creating or building things, whether it's carpentry, cooking, knitting, or any other craft that requires skill and dedication.
- **Mindfulness and Meditation:** Engaging in practices that promote self-awareness, inner peace, and connection to the present moment can be a source of meaning.
- **Legacy Building:** Some people find meaning in pursuing projects or initiatives that will have a lasting impact.

- **Personal Narratives:** Writing or documenting one's life story or experiences, understanding one's journey, and deriving meaning from past events can contribute to a sense of meaning.

The Benefits of Doing What's Meaningful

Here are some of the key benefits of doing what's meaningful to you:

- **Resilience and coping:** Finding meaning in life can enhance resilience and provide a buffer against stress and adversity. When faced with challenges, people with a strong sense of purpose and meaning are likelier to cope effectively, maintain optimism, and bounce back from setbacks.
- **Reduced psychological distress:** Engaging in meaningful activities has been associated with lower levels of psychological distress, including symptoms of depression, anxiety, and stress. Meaningful pursuits provide direction and motivation, which can help alleviate negative emotional states.
- **Enhanced self-esteem:** Having a sense of purpose and engaging in meaningful endeavors can boost self-esteem and self-worth. When people feel that their actions and contributions matter, it promotes a positive self-perception and a greater sense of personal value.
- **Increased motivation and engagement:** Meaningful activities often lead to higher intrinsic motivation and levels of engagement. When you pursue activities

aligned with your values and interests, you will likely experience a sense of fulfillment, enjoyment, and flow—a state of deep immersion and concentration in an activity.

- **Sense of identity and coherence:** Finding meaning in life helps you develop a coherent narrative. It provides a sense of identity and a framework for understanding your past, present, and future. This sense of coherence and narrative continuity contributes to a greater sense of self-understanding.
- **Improved quality of relationships:** Meaningful pursuits often involve connection and collaboration with others, leading to improved social relationships. Engaging in shared meaningful experiences can foster a sense of belonging, intimacy, and support.

Myths and Misunderstandings about Meaningful Engagement

It's important to dispel these myths and misconceptions to develop a more fulfilling and meaningful existence. Here are a few to consider:

Myth: Finding meaning requires a grand or extraordinary purpose.

Reality: A meaningful life need not involve achieving extraordinary goals or making a significant impact on a global scale. Meaning can be derived from a wide range of big and small activities. Engaging in everyday actions aligned with personal values and interests can bring a deep sense of purpose.

Myth: Meaning is a fixed destination.

Reality: Some people believe that once they find their life's purpose, it will remain unchanged. However, meaning is a dynamic and evolving concept. It can shift as we grow, encounter new experiences, and reassess our values and priorities. Finding meaning is an ongoing process.

Myth: External factors alone determine meaning.

Reality: Meaning in life does not solely rely on external circumstances, such as career success or social status. Although external factors can contribute to a sense of purpose, research indicates that internal factors, such as personal values, relationships, and engagement, play a significant role in finding meaning. Both internal and external factors shape one's sense of purpose.

Myth: Meaning is a universal concept.

Reality: Meaning in life is highly subjective and varies from person to person and culture to culture. What gives one person a deep sense of purpose may not resonate with another. People have unique values, interests, and life experiences that influence their search for meaning. What works in one culture will be meaningless in another. There is no single, universal path to finding meaning.

Myth: Finding meaning eliminates negative emotions.

Reality: Although living a meaningful life can enhance overall well-being, it doesn't eliminate negative emotions or life's challenges. Struggles and difficulties are a natural part of the human experience. However, having a sense of purpose and meaning can provide people with resilience and motivation to navigate difficult times and find greater fulfillment.

Myth: Meaning is a solitary pursuit.

Reality: Meaningful experiences often intertwine with our relationships and connections. The belief that finding meaning is a solitary journey overlooks the importance of social interactions and communal experiences. Sharing meaningful moments, engaging in acts of kindness, and nurturing relationships can deepen the sense of purpose and connectedness.

Self-Assessment for Doing What's Meaningful

The following questions help you assess your efforts to engage in activities that give your life meaning:

1. **Core Values:** What are my core values, and are my current activities aligned with them?
2. **Fulfillment:** Which activities make me feel most alive and fulfilled?
3. **Time Reflection:** Where am I investing most of my time and energy? Is this where I want to focus?
4. **Impact:** How are my activities positively impacting others or the world around me?

5. **Growth:** Am I learning and growing from the activities I'm engaging in? Are they challenging me in ways that promote personal growth?

6. **Legacy:** If I were to look back on my life many years from now, would I be proud of the activities I'm currently engaging in?

7. **Personal Freedom:** Do I surround myself with people and organizations that support those interests that provide a sense of personal purpose?

8. **Balance:** Do I feel balanced in the various activities I'm involved in, or is one area dominating the rest?

9. **Connection:** How connected do I feel to others in the activities I'm pursuing? Do these activities foster deep relationships and bonds?

10. **Vision and Goals:** Are my current activities moving me closer to my long-term goals and vision for my life?

11. **Feedback:** Do I get feedback from trusted friends, family, or mentors about the activities I'm engaging in?

12. **Re-evaluation:** When was the last time I sat down to re-evaluate the activities I'm involved in and their significance in my life?

Improving Skills and Abilities Related to Doing Meaningful Activities

Improving your ability to engage in meaningful activities often requires intentional reflection, planning, and action. Here are some strategies to help you enhance your capacity to do meaningful activities:

- **Self-reflect:** Take time to think about what truly matters to you. What are your values, passions, and life goals? Understanding these can guide you toward more meaningful activities.

- **Prioritize:** Sometimes, we must say "no" to certain tasks or obligations to make room for what's truly important. Learn to prioritize activities that align with your values and bring purpose to your life. Periodically assess how you're spending your time. This can help you realign your actions with your intentions.

- **Set Clear Goals:** Define clear, actionable goals for meaningful activities. This not only provides direction, but also a sense of accomplishment once achieved.

- **Manage Time Effectively:** Use time management tools and techniques, such as to-do lists, calendars, or time-blocking, to allocate dedicated time for meaningful activities.

- **Limit Distractions:** Reduce activities or habits that don't serve your larger purpose or drain your time without adding value, such as excessive social media use or aimless browsing.

- **Seek Mentorship:** Connect with people who exemplify a life filled with purpose and meaningful activities. They can provide guidance, inspiration, and practical advice.

- **Educate Yourself:** Attend workshops, read books, or take courses related to areas you find meaningful. Knowledge and skills can increase your impact and satisfaction in these areas.

- **Stay Flexible:** Although it's essential to plan, be open to change, too. Life is unpredictable, and sometimes detours lead to the most meaningful experiences.
- **Build a Support System:** Surround yourself with supportive friends, family, or community members who understand and share your quest for meaning. Meaningful relationships are a source of joy, support, and purpose. Invest time and energy in building and maintaining them.
- **Commit to Consistency:** Incorporate small, meaningful activities into your daily routine rather than occasional deep dives.
- **Practice Mindfulness:** Being present in the moment can enhance the depth and richness of any activity, making it more meaningful.
- **Volunteer:** Giving back often provides a profound sense of purpose. Find causes or organizations that resonate with your values.
- **Seek Feedback:** Sometimes, other people can offer valuable perspectives. Discuss your activities with trusted people to get insights about how you're spending your time.
- **Overcome Fear:** Don't let fear of the unknown or fear of failure prevent you from pursuing activities that could bring significant meaning to your life.
- **Celebrate Small Wins:** Recognizing and celebrating small achievements can motivate you to continue pursuing meaningful endeavors.

Books on Meaningful Engagement

The following books offer a mix of personal anecdotes, research, and actionable advice on understanding and acting with purpose. They can serve as valuable resources for anyone seeking to align their actions with their inner values and goals.

Leading for Purpose: How to Help Your People and Your Organization Benefit from the Pursuit of Meaning. Judd Allen and Donald Ardell explore how leaders and organizations can support peoples' sense of purpose.

Man's Search for Meaning. Psychiatrist Viktor Frankl draws on his experiences in Nazi concentration camps to discuss finding purpose even under the most trying of circumstances.

Essentialism: The Disciplined Pursuit of Less. Greg McKeown highlights the importance of focusing on what's essential in life and work and offers strategies to ensure we're dedicating our energies to what truly matters.

Start with Why: How Great Leaders Inspire Everyone to Take Action. Simon Sinek introduces the idea that successful individuals and organizations are clear about their "why"-- their purpose, cause, or belief.

Life on Purpose: How Living for What Matters Most Changes Everything. Victor Strecher explores the concept of having a clearly defined purpose in life and how it can significantly affect various aspects of health and well-being.

The Path Made Clear: Discovering Your Life's Direction and Purpose. Oprah Winfrey provides a collection of wisdom, insights, and anecdotes from her guests, illuminating the path to discovering purpose.

Chapter 20

Elevate Passion and Commitment

"Passion is energy. Feel the power that comes from focusing on what excites you."

- OPRAH WINFREY

"Commitment is what transforms a promise into reality."

- ABRAHAM LINCOLN

DO PASSION AND commitment play positive roles in your life? Passion and commitment are psychological states that reflect a deep involvement, dedication, and persistence toward a particular interest, goal, or activity. Passion and commitment are powerful motivational forces that fuel engagement and promote goal-directed behavior. They can provide a sense of purpose, direction, and fulfillment. However, when passion and commitment become obsessions and frustrations, they can lead to burnout and unhealthy coping mechanisms.

Cultures and subcultures deeply influence our choices, desires, and motivations. They provide the backdrop against which we discover and nurture our passions and lay down the paths we might feel committed to. As the world becomes more interconnected, people are often influenced by multiple subcultures, leading to a diverse and evolving landscape of passion and commitment. Here are some of the many ways cultural environments affect passions and commitments:

- Culture often defines what is valuable or important in a society. When people grow up in a culture that prizes certain values or beliefs, they might feel a stronger passion and commitment toward pursuits that align with those values. For example, people in cultures that highly value education might feel a greater commitment to academic achievement.

- Cultural heroes, figures, and icons are role models, influencing people's aspirations and passions. For instance, in a culture that celebrates entrepreneurs, people might be more passionate about starting their own businesses.

- Commitment and passion can be reinforced by what is tracked and communicated. Competitions (such as athletic races) and reviews (as would be offered by art critics) provide feedback. Such feedback can strengthen your commitment.

- Each culture has norms that identify important pursuits. These norms can guide individuals toward specific passions or commitments. For instance, certain family cultures have strong expectations to commit to family businesses.

- Cultural norms can also act as constraints, limiting the areas where passion and commitment are directed. For instance, in some cultures, pursuing a career in the arts might be frowned upon in favor of more "stable" professions.
- Shared cultural experiences can foster a collective passion and commitment through festivals, rituals, or ceremonies. For instance, participating in national Independence Day celebrations can evoke a strong sense of patriotic commitment.
- Every culture has stories, folklore, and narratives that instill values, morals, and ideals. These stories can inspire passion and commitment toward specific goals or paths. For example, Harriet Tubman made dangerous trips to lead around 70 enslaved individuals to freedom. This story can inspire women to help escape dangerous or unhealthy laws and conditions.
- Culture can provide the tools, resources, or platforms for people to explore their passions. For example, certain cultures might have rich traditions in arts or music, providing the infrastructure and resources for individuals to pursue those fields with commitment.
- A strong sense of belonging to a group or community can enhance commitment. When you feel part of something bigger, you often exhibit more passion and dedication to that group's goals or values.
- In many cultures, religious and spiritual beliefs guide people's passions and commitments. The values and tenets of a religion can shape what its followers are passionate about and where they commit their time and energy.

The Benefits of Passion and Commitment

A healthy degree of passion and commitment can offer the following benefits:

- **Enhanced resilience:** Passion and commitment can help you cope better with challenges and setbacks. Passion and commitment can help people to persevere, adapt their strategies, and maintain a positive mindset. This resilience can help protect against the negative impacts of stress and adversity on mental health.

- **Increased motivation:** Passion and commitment can provide a deep intrinsic drive to pursue goals and engage in activities you are passionate about. This internal motivation can sustain effort, persistence, and a positive attitude, leading to a greater likelihood of accomplishing tasks and achieving desired outcomes.

- **Flow experiences:** Experiencing passion and commitment can facilitate deep concentration, a sense of being fully absorbed in an activity. Such "flow experiences" are associated with increased enjoyment, improved performance, and optimal psychological functioning.

- **Reduced stress and burnout:** Engaging in activities or work that align with your passions can act as a buffer against stress and burnout. Passion and commitment provide a source of intrinsic motivation and enjoyment, counteracting the adverse effects of work-related stressors.

- **Improved self-esteem:** Achieving goals, mastering skills, and experiencing progress in areas of personal interest can reinforce a positive self-perception and self-worth.

- **Positive mood and happiness:** Engaging in activities aligned with your passions and demonstrating commitment to them can increase positive mood and happiness. Immersing yourself in activities you enjoy and care about generates positive emotions, fosters a sense of enjoyment, and contributes to an overall positive mood.

Myths and Misunderstandings about Passion and Commitment

The following myths or misunderstandings can undermine our capacity to benefit from passion and commitment:

Myth: Passion and commitment are innate traits; you either have them or don't have them.

Reality: Although some people may naturally be inclined towards certain interests or goals, passion, and commitment can also be developed and nurtured through personal exploration, experiences, and deliberate practice.

Myth: Passion and commitment guarantee constant motivation and enthusiasm.

Reality: Although passion and commitment can provide a strong motivational drive, they do not ensure a continuous state of motivation or enthusiasm. Like any other psychological state, passion and commitment can fluctuate over time and in response to various factors such as external circumstances, setbacks, or competing priorities. Sustaining motivation and enthusiasm requires ongoing effort and the ability to adapt to challenges.

Myth: Passion and commitment only apply to work or career-related pursuits.

Reality: Passion and commitment can be experienced in various domains of life, including hobbies, relationships, personal goals, and even everyday activities. People can feel passionate and committed to creative pursuits, sports, volunteering, parenting, and other areas of personal meaning and importance.

Myth: Passion and commitment always lead to success.

Reality: Although passion and commitment can increase the likelihood of success, they do not guarantee it. Factors influencing success include skills, opportunities, resources, and external circumstances. Passion and commitment provide the motivation and perseverance necessary for success but cannot solely determine the outcome.

Myth: Passion and commitment require sacrificing other areas of life.

Reality: A healthy and balanced approach to passion and commitment involves integrating them with other areas of life and maintaining overall well-being. Establishing boundaries, prioritizing self-care, and nurturing a holistic life balance is important.

Myth: Passion and commitment are fixed and unchanging.

Reality: Passion and commitment can evolve and change over time. As people grow, develop, and encounter new experiences, their passions and commitments may shift or expand. Flexibility and adaptability are key to maintaining a healthy relationship with passion and commitment.

Self-Assessment for Passion and Commitment

Regularly reflecting on your passions and commitments can help you align your commitments with your desires and motivations.

1. Am I pursuing any projects or goals that I feel excited and energized about?
2. Do I lose track of time when I'm engaged in these activities?
3. Am I willing to prioritize these passion-driven projects and goals over other activities or interests?
4. How do I respond to setbacks related to these pursuits? Do they deter me, or do they motivate me to work harder?
5. Am I consistently seeking to learn more or improve my skills associated with these passion-driven activities?
6. Can I visualize a future where I am deeply involved in this passion or commitment?
7. Do I push forward even when external motivators (like money or recognition) are absent?
8. Do I talk about this passion or commitment with others? Am I proud to share it?

9. Do I consistently return to this activity or goal, even after diversions or breaks?

10. Will I invest resources (like time, money, or energy) to further this passion or commitment?

11. When not directly engaged, how often do I think about this passion or commitment?

12. Am I willing to face challenges and step out of my comfort zone for passion or commitment?

13. Do I see these passions and activities as part of the legacy I wish to leave behind?

Improving Skills and Abilities Related to Passion and Commitment

Improving your capacity for passion and commitment is a continuous journey of self-discovery and refinement. It's about recognizing what fuels you, making deliberate choices to nurture that spark, and setting up systems and habits to sustain your momentum. Here are some steps to enhance your passion and commitment:

- **Self-Reflection:** Regularly take time for introspection to understand what genuinely excites and motivates you. Recognizing your core values and aligning them with your goals can boost your passion and commitment.
- **Set Clear Goals:** Defined goals can provide direction and purpose. Break them down into manageable tasks and celebrate small achievements.
- **Visualize Success:** Visualization techniques can foster a deeper emotional connection to your goals. Imagine the feelings and benefits of achieving your objectives.

- **Surround Yourself with Support:** Build a network of supportive friends, mentors, or colleagues who understand your passions and goals. They can provide encouragement, advice, and a sense of accountability.
- **Commit Publicly:** Sharing your goals with others can create a sense of accountability, making you more likely to follow through.
- **Prioritize Learning and Inspiration:** Invest in acquiring new skills and knowledge related to your passion. Continuous learning can reinvigorate your enthusiasm and deepen your commitment. Engage with books, podcasts, seminars, or workshops related to your passion. They can offer new perspectives and keep your enthusiasm alive.
- **Manage Time Effectively:** Allocate time to your passion or commitment. Tools like calendars, to-do lists, or time-tracking apps can help ensure you consistently devote time to your pursuits.
- **Seek Feedback:** Constructive feedback can help refine your approach and keep you on track. Seeing tangible progress can also reignite your passion.
- **Self-Care:** Ensure you care for your physical, emotional, and mental well-being. Passion and commitment can wane if you're exhausted or burnt out.
- **Re-evaluate Regularly:** Periodically assess your goals. It's okay to pivot or change direction if your passions change.
- **Commit to Consistency:** Even on days when passion feels low, showing up and maintaining consistency

can reignite your enthusiasm and strengthen your commitment muscle.

- **Limit Distractions:** Create an environment conducive to focusing on your passion. This might mean decluttering your workspace, setting specific times when you're unavailable, or using apps to block distractions.
- **Cultivate Resilience:** Develop your capacity to accept setbacks as part of the pathway to success. Developing a growth mindset can help you see challenges as learning opportunities rather than deterrents.
- **Practice Patience:** Recognize that passion and commitment often require time to yield results. Patience and persistence can be the difference between giving up and achieving your goals.

Books about Passion and Commitment

Books that delve into passion and commitment often address motivation, perseverance, and finding one's purpose. Here are some notable titles that provide insights on these topics:

Daring Greatly: How the Courage to Be Vulnerable Transforms the Way We Live, Love, Parent, and Lead. Brené Brown discusses the power of vulnerability in forging deeper connections, commitment, and finding one's true passion.

Grit: The Power of Passion and Perseverance. Angela Duckworth presents her research on "grit" — a combination of passion and perseverance — arguing that it's a more significant predictor of success than talent alone.

The Dip: A Little Book That Teaches You When to Quit (and When to Stick). Seth Godin discusses the challenges faced when pursuing a passion or commitment and how to determine when to persevere and when it's wise to quit.

Big Magic: Creative Living Beyond Fear. Elizabeth Gilbert shares her insights on the nature of inspiration, creativity, and the challenges and joys of the creative process, urging readers to embrace their passions without fear.

Mastery. Robert Greene explores the journey of achieving mastery in one's field, discussing the phases of learning, the importance of mentorship, and the role of deep passion and commitment.

Drive: The Surprising Truth About What Motivates Us. Daniel Pink explores the psychology of motivation, arguing that autonomy, mastery, and purpose are the primary drivers of human behavior rather than external rewards.

The Element: How Finding Your Passion Changes Everything. Ken Robinson and Lou Aronica argue that finding one's "element" — the point where natural talent meets personal passion — can transform a person's life.

Find Your Why: A Practical Guide for Discovering Purpose for You and Your Team. Simon Sinek, David Mead, and Peter Docker guide individuals and organizations to discover their "Why"--the purpose and passion that drives them.

Start with Why: How Great Leaders Inspire Everyone to Take Action. Simon Sinek examines how individuals and organizations can achieve more by focusing on "why" they do what they do rather than just "how" or "what."

The Passion Paradox: A Guide to Going All In, Finding Success, and Discovering the Benefits of an Unbalanced Life. Brad Stulberg and Steve Magness delve into the duality of passion, discussing its benefits while cautioning against its potential downsides.

Proactive Mental Health Building Block
Safety

Mental health is inextricably linked with financial, emotional, and physical safety. Safety in these domains can act as a protective factor, mitigating the risk of developing mental health disorders. Conversely, the absence of safety can be a significant stressor, increasing the risk of mental health issues. Ensuring well-being requires an integrated approach that addresses not just our mental health but also our financial, emotional, and physical safety.

The following chapters address financial, physical, and emotional safety. The relationship between mental health and these forms of safety is intricate and multifaceted. Each aspect can influence and be influenced by mental health, either directly or indirectly. Here's how:

Financial Safety and Mental Health

- **Direct Effects:** Economic instability or poverty can lead to chronic stress, anxiety, and depression. Those struggling financially may constantly worry about affording necessities, which can deteriorate mental well-being. Financial strain can lead to other hardships, like housing instability or food insecurity, further aggravating mental health issues.
- **Protective Role:** Actions that achieve financial security, such as employment, high-quality housing, a financial safety net, and the wherewithal to participate in leisure activities, play a positive role in well-being.
- **Reciprocal Relationship:** Mental health disorders can also make it more challenging for people to maintain steady employment or manage finances, creating a cycle of financial instability.

Emotional Safety and Mental Health

- **Direct Effects:** Emotional abuse, neglect, or chronic exposure to hostile environments can lead to mental health conditions like depression, anxiety, post-traumatic stress disorder (PTSD), and other mood disorders.

- **Protective Role:** A positive emotional environment, characterized by supportive relationships and affirmation, can act as a buffer against mental health disorders. Emotional support helps people be resilient during challenging times.
- **Connections:** Mental health conditions might also affect people's perception of emotional safety. For example, someone with anxiety might perceive environments as more threatening or hostile than they are.

Physical Safety and Mental Health

- **Direct Effects:** Experiencing physical harm or living in an environment where physical safety is threatened can lead to various mental health disorders, including PTSD, anxiety, and depression. Injuries or chronic health conditions can impact mental health.
- **Protective Role:** Healthy physical environments protect against accidents and harm and support healthy behaviors like sleep, physical activity, and social engagement. These outcomes are important to maintaining mental health and well-being.
- **Connections:** Mental health conditions can influence people's perception of physical safety. For instance, people with certain disorders, such as paranoia, might feel unsafe even in non-threatening environments.

How Culture Supports or Undermines Safety

Culture plays a significant role in shaping our perceptions of physical, financial, and emotional safety. Its influence can be both supportive and undermining in various ways:

Supportive Aspects of Culture

- **Social Cohesion:** In cultures emphasizing community and social bonds, people often feel more emotional safety due to the available support networks.
- **Shared Values and Norms:** A shared set of ethical or moral guidelines can make people feel physically safer because they know that similar principles guide most people in their community.
- **Economic Support Systems:** In cultures that value economic solidarity, there might be stronger social safety nets, workers' rights, and community funds to support people experiencing financial hardship.
- **Emotional Literacy:** Some cultures prioritize kindness and open communication, which can foster environments where people feel emotionally secure and understood.
- **Resilience and Coping Mechanisms:** Cultures with a history of overcoming hardship often have built-in coping mechanisms that can be supportive in times of individual or community crisis.
- **Recognition of Individual Worth:** Cultures that emphasize the intrinsic value of each person can support emotional safety by reducing the stigma associated with mental health challenges or financial hardship.

Undermining Aspects of Culture

- **Stigma and Discrimination:** In some cultures, there may be deeply ingrained prejudices against certain groups, affecting these people's emotional, financial, and sometimes physical safety.
- **Toxic Masculinity/Femininity:** Stereotypes about what constitutes "real" manhood or womanhood can lead to emotional suppression and unhealthy behaviors, affecting emotional safety and overall well-being.
- **Financial Inequality:** Cultures that strongly emphasize individual success may undermine financial safety through a lack of support systems for those who are struggling.
- **Collectivist Pressure:** In highly collectivist cultures, the pressure to conform can lead to emotional stress and, in some cases, physical risk if individuals deviate from societal expectations.
- **Lack of Mental Health Awareness:** Cultures stigmatizing mental health issues can undermine emotional safety, as people in need may avoid seeking help.
- **Violent Norms:** In some cultures, physical violence is normalized or accepted as a means to express oneself or resolve conflict, significantly undermining physical safety.
- **Perception of Vulnerability:** In some cultures, seeking help may be perceived as a weakness, making it difficult for individuals to secure emotional or physical safety.

Chapter 21

Achieve Financial Security

"Anyone who has ever struggled with poverty knows how extremely expensive it is to be poor."

- JAMES BALDWIN

"Financial security provides you with the opportunity to enjoy life to the fullest, without the constant worry of how to pay your bills."

- SUZE ORMAN

FINANCIAL SECURITY REFERS to having a stable income or other resources to support a basic standard of living now and in the foreseeable future. Key elements of financial security include:

- **Stable Income:** Having a consistent and reliable source of income that is sufficient to cover basic living expenses, such as food, housing, and health care.

- **Employment Security:** Being reasonably protected against unemployment and having access to assistance or opportunities to find new employment if unemployed.
- **Health Security:** Having access to health care and the ability to afford it, including health insurance coverage.
- **Savings and Investments:** The ability to save money for future needs, emergencies, retirement, and other long-term goals.
- **Social Safety Nets:** Access to social welfare programs or other forms of assistance in times of need, including unemployment benefits, social security, and food assistance programs.
- **Asset Security:** Owning assets, like a home or business, can provide stability and growth opportunities.
- **Debt Management:** The ability to manage debts so that debt doesn't threaten financial stability.
- **Retirement Security:** Having resources, savings, or pension plans to maintain a decent standard of living during retirement.

Financial security is often portrayed as a marker of success and competence. People are bombarded with messages that equate financial success with personal worth and happiness. When they struggle to achieve financial security, people may perceive themselves as inadequate or failures, triggering feelings of shame. When they perceive themselves as falling short compared to others, it can intensify feelings of shame and inadequacy. Such shame can be widespread when there are large income disparities and when people compare their financial success with celebrities. Some people may cope with their shame by engaging in unhealthy financial behaviors, such as overspending, taking on excessive debt, or pursuing risky financial ventures to prove their worth. These coping mechanisms can further exacerbate financial insecurity and shame.

Historical and systemic discrimination has created disparities in educational and employment opportunities. These disparities can limit access to well-paying jobs and opportunities for financial advancement. These disparities also contribute to financial insecurity.

Economic cycles can significantly contribute to financial insecurity:

- During economic downturns or recessions, many businesses cut costs by laying off employees.
- Economic downturns can result in declining stock markets and reduced investment returns.
- Housing prices can be significantly affected by economic cycles. During economic booms, housing costs may rise rapidly, making it difficult for people to afford homes or rent. Conversely, housing market crashes can lead to negative equity for homeowners, impacting their financial well-being.
- Economic cycles influence consumer confidence. During economic downturns, people tend to cut back on spending and may delay major purchases, affecting businesses and job opportunities.
- Economic downturns make it difficult for people to meet their debt obligations.
- During economic downturns, lenders may tighten their lending criteria, making it harder for people to access credit when they need it most.

The Benefits of Financial Security

Financial security can significantly promote positive mental health outcomes by providing stability, control, access to resources, and opportunities for growth and support. It can:

- **Reduce Stress and Anxiety:** Financial security provides stability, reducing financial stressors and anxiety related to meeting basic needs. Knowing you can cover essential expenses such as housing, food, and healthcare promotes a sense of security and peace of mind, lowering chronic stress and anxiety.

- **Enhance the Sense of Control:** Having the financial resources to make choices and pursue opportunities fosters a sense of autonomy and empowerment. This increased control can positively impact mental health by promoting feelings of self-efficacy and reducing helplessness.

- **Improve Access to Healthcare:** The financial means to afford therapy, medications, or other treatments can enhance mental well-being by ensuring timely and appropriate care. Access to healthcare resources contributes to early intervention, symptom management, and overall better mental health outcomes.

- **Increase Social Support:** Individuals with stable financial situations often have better access to social networks and resources. Strong social support is a protective factor for mental health, as it provides emotional support, practical assistance, and a sense of belonging, which can buffer against stress and improve overall well-being.

- **Increase Personal Growth:** Financial security allows individuals to invest in education, skills training, or personal interests, enhancing self-esteem, confidence, and a sense of purpose. These factors contribute to positive mental health outcomes and overall life satisfaction.
- **Improve Work-Life Balance:** Financial security may provide the means to secure stable employment, negotiate flexible working hours, or pursue career opportunities aligned with personal values and interests. Achieving a healthy balance between work and personal life promotes mental well-being and reduces the risk of burnout or work-related stress.

Myths and Misunderstandings about Financial Security

The following myths or misunderstandings can undermine our capacity to achieve financial security:

Myth: Financial security guarantees good mental health.

Reality: Although financial security is undoubtedly important, mental health is influenced by multiple factors, including genetics, social support, personal resilience, and access to mental healthcare.

Myth: Financial security is solely the responsibility of individuals.

Reality: Financial security involves individual choices, but it is also influenced by broader systemic factors such as financial policies, labor markets, education systems, and social inequalities. Recognizing the structural determinants of financial security is crucial for developing effective interventions and promoting mental well-being at a societal level.

Myth: Financial security is only about money.

Reality: Although financial stability is a significant aspect of financial security, factors like job security, access to healthcare, and social safety nets are also major contributors.

Myth: You must earn big to invest.

Reality: Small investments grow over time. Many modern investment platforms allow for small initial investments, making them accessible to almost everyone.

Myth: Only financial professionals can understand investments.

Reality: Although financial professionals can provide valuable insights, you can understand investments and manage your portfolio with the many resources available today.

Myth: Higher income equals financial security.

Reality: Financial security is not about how much money you have, but how you manage, save, and invest it. It's possible for someone with a high income to live paycheck to paycheck if they have poor financial habits.

Myth: All debt is bad.

Reality: Not all debt is created equal. Although high-interest debt (like credit card debt) should be avoided or paid off quickly, taking on strategic debt, like mortgages or student loans, can be seen as an investment in one's future.

Self-Assessment for Financial Security

The following questions can help you assess your financial situation and provide insights into areas requiring attention or improvement.

1. Do you have a stable job or income source?
2. Does your current occupation or industry offer growth and advancement opportunities?
3. Do you have savings or emergency funds to handle unexpected expenses or financial emergencies?
4. Can your savings cover at least three to six months of living expenses?
5. Are you managing your debt effectively, making timely payments, and controlling debt levels?
6. Are your housing costs, including rent or mortgage payments, utilities, and maintenance, affordable within your income?
7. Can you comfortably meet basic needs like food, transportation, and healthcare?
8. Are you on track to secure your financial future in retirement?
9. Do you have adequate insurance coverage, such as health insurance, disability insurance, or life insurance?

10. Do you have a supportive network of family, friends, financial professionals, or community resources to assist with financial decisions?

Improving Your Financial Security

Achieving and maintaining financial security is a life-long process. It requires consistent effort, discipline, and sometimes sacrifice. Here are some of the strategies you can use to increase your financial security:

Stay Employed:

- Find a career and job that matches your skills, interests, and abilities.
- Enhance your job security by being indispensable at work.
- Acquire new skills or certifications that are in demand.
- Stay updated with industry trends.
- Increase your capacity to communicate, problem-solve, and adapt.

Budget and Save:

- Track expenses: Use tools or apps to monitor where your money is going.
- Set a budget: Allocate funds for necessities, savings, and leisure. Stick to it.
- Automate savings: Set up automatic transfers to a savings account.

Live Below Your Means:

- Prioritize needs over wants.
- Look for ways to cut unnecessary expenses.

Create an Emergency Fund:

- Start by saving for 3-6 months of expenses, then expand as you see fit. This fund can be a cushion against unexpected costs or job losses.

Homeownership:

- Under the right circumstances, owning property can be a long-term investment and provide housing security.

Develop Multiple Sources of Income:

- Consider part-time jobs, freelancing, or opportunities for passive income.
- Start investing—even small amounts--to capitalize on the power of compound interest.
- Diversify investments to spread and reduce risk.

Reduce Debt:

- Prioritize paying off high-interest debts like credit card balances.
- Avoid accumulating more debt.
- Consider debt consolidation or refinancing options if they suit your situation.

Build a Network:

- Networking can open doors to job opportunities and business ventures.
- Join professional associations or community groups.
- Engage with financial planners, accountants, or other experts as needed.

Insure:

- Purchase adequate health, life, disability, and property insurance.
- Regularly review and update your coverage.

Plan for Retirement:

- Contribute to retirement accounts like 401(k) or IRAs.
- Regularly review and adjust your retirement strategies based on age and financial goals.

Avoid Financial Scams:

- Stay informed about common scams.
- Be skeptical of offers that seem too good to be true.

Establish Good Credit:

- Pay bills on time.
- Monitor your credit report for errors or fraudulent activity.

Books about Financial Security

Here are some books that discuss the intersection of financial security and mental health, as well as strategies for achieving financial security:

Evicted: Poverty and Profit in the American City. Matthew Desmond explores the effects of eviction and financial instability on mental health and overall well-being by sharing the stories of eight families in Milwaukee.

$2.00 a Day: Living on Almost Nothing in America. Kathryn Edin and H. Luke Shaefer document the lives of families living in extreme poverty in the U.S., exploring the emotional and psychological toll of such financial conditions.

Nickel and Dimed: On (Not) Getting By in America. Barbara Ehrenreich goes undercover to explore the lives of low-wage workers in the U.S., offering a profound look into financial insecurity.

The Financial Diet: A Total Beginner's Guide to Getting Good with Money. Chelsea Fagan discusses personal finance and provides strategies for a healthier financial mindset.

Mind Over Money: Overcoming the Money Disorders That Threaten Our Financial Health. Brad Klontz and Ted Klontz dive deep into people's emotional and psychological relationship with money, exploring financial anxiety, money avoidance, and money worship.

Scarcity: Why Having Too Little Means So Much. Sendhil Mullainathan and Eldar Shafir delve into the psychological and cognitive effects of scarcity, whether it's a lack of time, money, or resources, and how this impacts decision-making.

When She Makes More: 10 Rules for Breadwinning Women. Farnoosh Torabi addresses the unique challenges faced by women who are the primary earners in their households. This book touches on the emotional and psychological implications of these dynamics.

Chapter 22

Avoid and Stop Physical and Emotional Abuse

"Hurt people hurt people. We are not being judgmental by separating ourselves from such people. But we should do so with compassion."

— WILL BOWEN

"Emotional violence is another kind of abuse ... it's not about words because an emotionally abusive person doesn't always resort to using the verbal club, but rather the verbal untraceable poison."

— AUGUSTEN BURROUGHS

EMOTIONAL AND PHYSICAL abuse are two forms of abuse that people might encounter in various contexts, such as relationships, families, or social environments. They can coexist; indeed, someone subjected to physical abuse often experiences emotional abuse. Avoiding and stopping emotional or physical abuse is vital for your well-being and the health of relationships, families, and societies.

Emotional abuse doesn't necessarily involve physical contact. Examples of emotional abuse include:

- Verbal abuse (insults, belittling comments, name-calling)
- Manipulation
- Threats of harm
- Humiliation or shaming
- Isolation from friends or family
- Controlling behaviors, including monitoring someone's movements or dictating their choices
- Withholding affection or emotional support as a form of punishment

Physical abuse involves using force against another person, resulting in bodily harm or injury. It can range from mild forms to severe acts that can lead to serious injuries or even death.

Examples include:

- Hitting, slapping, punching
- Pushing or shoving
- Kicking
- Choking or strangulation
- Using weapons
- Physical restraint against one's will

The Benefits of Avoiding or Stopping Physical or Emotional Abuse

Important benefits are linked to being free from physical and emotional violence and abuse. These benefits are supported by research and emphasize the importance of a safe and nurturing environment for one's psychological well-being. Here are some key mental health benefits:

- Being free from violence and abuse significantly decreases the risk of developing or exacerbating symptoms of anxiety and depression. Removing constant threats, fear, and distressing experiences allows people to experience greater safety and stability, improving mental health outcomes.

- Physical and emotional abuse can severely erode people's self-esteem and self-worth. Leaving an abusive environment or relationship enables people to rebuild their self-concept and regain confidence in their abilities, strengths, and worthiness. This improved self-perception contributes to enhanced overall well-being.

- Violence and abuse often disrupt emotional regulation, leading to emotional dysregulation and heightened reactivity. By being free from these traumatic experiences, people can gradually regain their ability to manage and regulate their emotions effectively. This fosters emotional stability, resilience, and adaptive coping strategies.

- Survivors of violence and abuse often experience a loss of control and agency over their lives. Breaking free from these harmful situations allows them to regain control, autonomy, and empowerment.

- Healing from violence and abuse opens the possibility of developing healthy and supportive relationships. Being in a safe environment allows people to learn and practice positive communication skills, establish boundaries, and build trusting connections with others. This fosters a sense of belonging and contributes to improved interpersonal functioning.

- Violence and abuse often lead to the development of post-traumatic stress symptoms. Being free from these traumatic experiences allows the healing process to begin. Over time, people may experience reduced symptoms such as intrusive thoughts, nightmares, and hypervigilance.

- When free from violence and abuse, people can focus on personal growth, pursue their goals and aspirations, and engage in activities that bring them joy and fulfillment.

Skills and Abilities for Ending Physical and Emotional Abuse

Avoiding or stopping emotional or physical abuse is vital for individual well-being and the health of relationships, families, and societies. It requires concerted efforts at all levels, from personal to societal, to effectively address the root causes and manifestations of abuse.

On a Personal Level:

- Understanding the early signs of emotional or physical abuse can help people avoid or end a potentially harmful relationship or situation. Such signs could include excessive jealousy, attempts to control or isolate, belittling language, etc.

- Setting clear personal boundaries and communicating them can sometimes deter abusive behaviors.
- Confiding in trusted individuals or seeking professional help can guide and support people who are at risk of or dealing with emotional or physical abuse.
- When possible, removing yourself from people and places that are abusive is very important.

On a Relationship Level:

- Open and effective communication may help address concerns before they escalate into emotionally or physically abusive situations.
- Couples or family therapy can provide tools and strategies to address underlying issues and change harmful behaviors.
- Having a safety plan is crucial for people to be prepared to leave if abuse occurs or escalates.

On Community and Societal Levels:

- Public awareness campaigns can highlight the signs of emotional and physical abuse and promote healthy relationships.
- Implementing and enforcing laws against abuse and violence can deter potential abusers and protect victims.

- Offering accessible helplines, shelters, and counseling services for victims can make a difference in both preventing and stopping abuse and violence.
- Implementing educational programs in schools and communities that teach about consent, healthy relationships, and conflict resolution can help in the long term.

For Potential Perpetrators:

- Recognizing harmful behaviors and tendencies is the first step toward change.
- Before things escalate, those who fear they might become emotionally or physically abusive should seek therapy or counseling to address their behaviors.
- Taking responsibility for abusive actions and seeking to make amends can be part of the healing process.

Myths and Misunderstandings about Physical and Emotional Abuse

Prevalent myths can get in the way of better understanding the complexities of violence and abuse and working towards creating a supportive and safe environment for ourselves and others.

Myth: If it's not physical, it's not abuse.

Reality: Abuse can take various forms, including physical, emotional, verbal, sexual, and financial. Emotional and psychological abuse, such as manipulation, threats, or controlling behavior, can be equally harmful and leave lasting scars, even though they may not be as visible as physical abuse.

Myth: Abuse only happens in certain demographics or socioeconomic groups.

Reality: Abuse can occur across all demographics and socioeconomic groups. It transcends boundaries such as race, ethnicity, religion, social status, and education. Recognizing that anyone can be a perpetrator or victim of abuse is important, and no one is immune to its effects.

Myth: Victims can easily leave abusive relationships.

Reality: Leaving an abusive relationship is often very challenging and complicated. Victims may face numerous barriers, including fear, financial dependence, lack of support networks, and potential retaliation from the abuser. It is crucial to understand the complexities involved and provide appropriate support and resources to facilitate the process of leaving safely.

Myth: Abuse is easy to detect.

Reality: Not all forms of abuse leave visible marks. Emotional and psychological abuse can be insidious and leave deep emotional wounds without leaving any external signs. Recognizing and addressing non-physical forms of abuse requires attentiveness to behavioral patterns, emotional well-being, and changes in the victim's demeanor.

Myth: Abuse is a private matter; outsiders should not get involved.

Reality: Abuse is not a private matter but a societal issue that affects individuals, families, and communities. It is crucial to intervene and support victims to break the cycle of abuse. By promoting awareness, challenging societal attitudes, and providing resources, we can create a safer environment and help those affected by abuse.

Myth: Once the abuse stops, the effects disappear.

Reality: The effects of abuse can be long-lasting and impact various aspects of a person's life. Survivors may experience psychological, emotional, and physical repercussions even after the abuse ends. Healing and recovery often require ongoing support, therapy, and rebuilding one's sense of self and safety.

Myth: Abuse only affects the victim; it doesn't impact others.

Reality: Abuse can have far-reaching effects on victims, their family members, friends, and the broader community. Witnessing abuse or growing up in an abusive environment can have lasting consequences on children, perpetuating the cycle of abuse. Addressing abuse requires a holistic approach, considering the well-being of all those affected.

Self-Assessment for Physical and Emotional Abuse

Determining whether you are free from abuse can be challenging. If you find it hard to navigate the following questions independently, seeking help from a qualified mental health professional can provide additional support, guidance, and insights.

1. Am I free from physical harm, threats, or acts of violence?
2. Do I feel safe in my environment and relationships?
3. Are there any ongoing patterns of physical aggression or harm in my life?
4. Do I feel safe expressing my emotions without fear of retaliation or punishment?
5. Can I set and maintain healthy boundaries within my relationships?
6. Do I experience freedom from manipulation, control, or coercive behaviors in my interactions with others?
7. Can I make choices without fear of retribution or punishment?

Books on Mental Health and Abuse

Books that address avoiding or stopping physical and emotional abuse often focus on understanding the roots of abuse, strategies for intervention, and ways to build healthier relationships.

Why Does He Do That?: Inside the Minds of Angry and Controlling Men. Lundy Bancroft writes about the patterns and mindsets of abusive men, offering insights for those affected by such behavior.

The Batterer as Parent: Addressing the Impact of Domestic Violence on Family Dynamics. Lundy Bancroft and Jay Silverman delve into the effects of domestic violence on children and parenting.

The Gift of Fear: Survival Signals That Protect Us from Violence. Gavin de Becker teaches readers to trust their instincts and recognize signs of potential violence.

The Verbally Abusive Relationship: How to Recognize It and How to Respond. Patricia Evans provides insights into verbal abuse, helping victims recognize signs and strategies to cope or exit such relationships.

Trauma and Recovery: The Aftermath of Violence – From Domestic Abuse to Political Terror. Judith Lewis Herman discusses the profound impact of trauma and the path to recovery.

The Macho Paradox: Why Some Men Hurt Women and How All Men Can Help. Jackson Katz offers a perspective on male violence against women, focusing on cultural norms and how men can be a part of the solution.

The Body Keeps the Score: Brain, Mind, and Body in the Healing of Trauma. Bessel van der Kolk explains how untreated trauma can sometimes manifest as aggression or violent behavior.

In Love and In Danger: A Teen's Guide to Breaking Free of Abusive Relationships. Barrie Levy offers teens guidance on recognizing and breaking free from abusive relationships.

Nonviolent Communication: A Language of Life. Marshall Rosenberg offers a powerful methodology for ensuring compassionate communication, which can prevent and heal emotional harm in personal and professional relationships.

Chapter 23

Spend Time in Healthy Physical Environments

"The environment is where we all meet; where we all have a mutual interest; it is the one thing all of us share."
—LADY BIRD JOHNSON

"We shape our buildings; thereafter they shape us."
—WINSTON CHURCHILL

HEALTHY PHYSICAL ENVIRONMENTS foster wellness, reduce potential risks, and make daily activities pleasant and rejuvenating. Over time, living, working, learning, and playing in such environments contribute significantly to our quality of life and mental health. Here's what various healthy environments might encompass:

Healthy Living Environment:

- **Shelter:** A safe and secure home that protects from adverse weather conditions and potential threats.
- **Clean Air:** Minimal pollution, with good ventilation and possibly the presence of air-purifying plants or devices.
- **Access to Clean Water:** Safe for drinking and daily use.
- **Safe Food:** Storage and preparation areas that minimize the risk of foodborne illnesses.
- **Hygiene:** Facilities for regular cleaning and bathing.
- **Limitation of Toxins:** Absence or minimal use of harmful chemicals in cleaning supplies, paints, and other household items.

Healthy Work or School Environment:

- **Ergonomics:** Furniture and equipment that supports the body and reduces strain or injury.
- **Proper Lighting:** Adequate natural and artificial lighting that reduces eye strain and boosts mood.
- **Safe Conditions:** Environments free from hazards, with protocols in place to handle emergencies.
- **Good Air Quality:** Ventilation systems that reduce pollutants and maintain good airflow.
- **Break Areas:** Spaces to rest, eat, and recuperate away from workstations.
- **Green Spaces:** If possible, areas with plants or proximity to outdoor spaces for relaxation and fresh air.

Healthy Recreational Environment:

- **Safe Recreational Areas:** Playgrounds, parks, and recreational facilities that are well-maintained and free from hazards.
- **Access to Nature:** Opportunities to engage with natural environments to reduce stress and increase well-being.
- **Clean and Safe Water:** For activities like swimming, boating, or fishing.
- **Community Engagement:** Spaces that promote social interaction, community bonding, and cultural expression.
- **Equipment & Facilities:** Well-maintained and safe equipment for various recreational activities.

Benefits of Spending Time in Healthy Environments

Here are the mental health benefits associated with living, working, learning, and playing in healthy physical environments:

- **Reduced Stress and Anxiety:** Healthy physical environments, such as those with access to nature or green spaces, have been consistently linked to reduced stress and anxiety levels. Exposure to natural elements, such as plants, trees, and water, including indoors, helps promote relaxation and reduce stress.
- **Improved Mood:** Elements like natural light, attractive surroundings, and pleasant aesthetics have been shown to positively influence mood, increasing feel-

ings of happiness, contentment, and overall psychological well-being.

- **Enhanced Cognitive Function:** Healthy physical environments can improve cognitive function and performance. Well-lit spaces, proper ventilation, and comfortable temperatures optimize cognitive abilities, such as attention, memory, and problem-solving. In contrast, poor environmental conditions, such as excessive noise or inadequate lighting, can impair cognitive functioning and increase mental fatigue.

- **Increased Productivity and Concentration:** Well-designed environments with features like good lighting, ergonomic furniture, and optimal noise levels positively impact productivity and concentration. People in healthy physical environments are more likely to experience higher job satisfaction, engagement, and improved focus, leading to enhanced performance.

- **Boosted Creativity:** Certain physical environments, such as natural landscapes or aesthetically stimulating spaces, can foster creativity and innovation. Exposure to nature or engaging in activities in visually interesting surroundings can stimulate the imagination, promote divergent thinking, and enhance creative problem-solving abilities.

- **Improved Sleep Quality:** Factors such as comfortable temperatures, low noise levels, and access to fresh air promote better sleep hygiene, leading to more restorative and rejuvenating sleep. Good sleep positively impacts mood regulation, cognitive functioning, and overall mental well-being.

- **Sense of Connection and Community:** Accessible and inviting spaces encourage social interactions, support social cohesion, and reduce feelings of isolation or loneliness, all of which benefit mental health and well-being.

Myths and Misunderstandings about Healthy Physical Environments

Several myths or misunderstandings exist about healthy physical environments.

Myth: Healthy physical environments are solely about cleanliness and hygiene.

Reality: Although cleanliness and hygiene are essential aspects of healthy environments, they are not the only factors. A healthy physical environment encompasses a broader range of elements, including lighting, ventilation, access to nature, ergonomic design, and overall aesthetics. It considers the psychological, emotional, and social well-being of individuals in addition to physical health.

Myth: Physical environment has minimal impact on mental health and well-being.

Reality: Research consistently demonstrates that the physical environment significantly influences mental health and well-being. Factors such as exposure to natural elements, access to green spaces, presence of natural light, and noise reduction can profoundly impact mood, stress levels, cognitive function, and overall psychological well-being. Ignoring the importance of the physical environment in mental health can undermine the potential for positive outcomes.

Myth: A one-size-fits-all approach works for designing healthy physical environments.

Reality: Designing healthy physical environments requires consideration of individual and contextual factors. People have diverse preferences, needs, and sensitivities to environmental stimuli. Cultural, socioeconomic, and developmental factors also play a role. A one-size-fits-all approach neglects the importance of customization, inclusivity, and tailoring environments to accommodate diverse populations and their specific requirements.

Myth: Healthy physical environments are solely the responsibility of individuals.

Reality: Although individuals have a role in creating and maintaining healthy environments, the responsibility also lies with leaders, policymakers, urban planners, employers, and designers. System-level changes, such as implementing sustainable practices, providing accessible public spaces, and designing workplaces prioritizing employee well-being, are essential. Collective action and structural changes are necessary to ensure healthy physical environments are available and accessible.

Myth: Healthy physical environments are expensive.

Reality: Although certain aspects of healthy environments may involve costs, creating positive physical environments doesn't always require substantial financial investments. Simple interventions like incorporating plants, optimizing natural lighting, improving indoor air quality, and ensuring ergonomic designs can often be achieved with modest resources. Furthermore, investing in healthy environments can lead to long-term cost savings by promoting well-being, reducing healthcare expenses, and enhancing productivity.

Assessing Supportive Physical Environments

The following questions help determine whether you live, work, learn, and play in healthy physical environments.

Living Environment:

1. Do I feel physically comfortable in my living space regarding temperature, lighting, and ventilation?
2. Does my living environment provide me with safety and security?
3. Are there opportunities for privacy and personal space in my living environment?
4. Do I have access to natural light and views of nature from within my living space?

Working Environment:

1. Does my workplace provide a comfortable, ergonomic workstation that supports good posture and reduces physical strain?

2. Is the lighting in my workplace adequate and free from excessive glare?
3. Does my workplace offer opportunities for natural light and views of the outdoors?
4. Are noise levels in my workplace at a manageable and non-disruptive level?
5. Does my workplace foster community, collaboration, and social interaction?

Recreational Environment:

1. Do I have access to outdoor or recreational areas to engage in physical activities or connect with nature?
2. Are there opportunities for play and leisure that align with my interests and preferences?
3. Does my recreational environment promote relaxation, stress reduction, and enjoyment?
4. Do I feel a sense of safety and comfort in my recreational spaces?

Actions for Finding or Creating Healthier Personal Environments

Finding and creating healthier environments for work, rest, learning, and play requires a combination of individual actions, collaborative efforts, and sometimes institutional changes. Here are actions tailored to each context:

For Work and Learning:

- **Ergonomics:** Invest in ergonomic furniture and equipment. This can include standing desks, supportive chairs, and computer screen risers to ensure screens are at eye level.

- **Natural Lighting:** Utilize natural light whenever possible. Arrange workspaces near windows and use sheer curtains to diffuse light without blocking it.
- **Indoor Plants:** Incorporate plants into the space. They purify the air and also have psychological benefits.
- **Regular Breaks:** Encourage regular breaks to stretch, hydrate, and rest the eyes from screens.
- **Noise Management:** Use noise-canceling headphones, white noise machines, or partitions to reduce distractions in noisy environments.
- **Clutter Management:** Organize and declutter spaces regularly. A tidy environment can enhance productivity and reduce stress.
- **Digital Hygiene:** Ensure computer software is updated and emails are organized. Reduce digital clutter to enhance focus.
- **Promote Work-Life Balance:** Establish boundaries for work hours and encourage employees to fully disengage after work.

For Rest:

- **Comfortable Bedding:** Invest in a quality mattress, supportive pillows, and comfortable bedding.
- **Dim Lighting:** Use soft, warm lights in the evening. Consider using blackout curtains for uninterrupted sleep.
- **Temperature Control:** Maintain a comfortable room temperature, usually cooler, for better sleep.

- **Minimize Electronics:** Limit screen time before bed. The blue light from devices can interfere with sleep.
- **Calm Environment:** Consider using diffusers with calming essential oils, playing soft music, or using white noise machines to create a serene environment.
- **Reading:** Encourage reading physical books (rather than screens) before bed to wind down.

For Recreation:

- **Green Spaces:** Advocate for or create green spaces in your community. Parks, gardens, and even small green patches can make a difference.
- **Safe Recreational Areas:** Ensure these areas are safe and free from hazards.
- **Engage in Group Activities:** Promote group activities like team sports, group hikes, or community gatherings. Social interactions can be rejuvenating.
- **Limit Screen Time:** Encourage more physical activities and less time on electronic devices. This can include board games, outdoor sports, or crafting.
- **Promote Cultural and Artistic Activities:** Engage in or organize events related to art, music, dance, or other cultural activities. They're not only fun but also mentally stimulating.
- **Variety:** Regularly change up leisure activities to prevent monotony and stimulate different parts of the brain and body.

Across All Environments:

- **Promote Sustainability:** Reduce waste, recycle, and support eco-friendly initiatives. Consider energy-efficient appliances and fixtures.
- **Improve Air Quality:** Regularly clean and spaces. Use air purifiers if necessary.
- **Accessibility:** Ensure that spaces are accessible to everyone, including those with disabilities.
- **Community Engagement:** Engage with neighbors and community members. A sense of community can improve mental well-being and foster collaborative efforts for healthier spaces.

Books About Healthy Physical Environments

Here's a list of books that touch on creating healthy personal environments:

Joyful: The Surprising Power of Ordinary Things to Create Extraordinary Happiness. Ingrid Fetell Lee discusses the aesthetics of joy and how the environment around us, including its design and color, can significantly impact our mood and well-being.

Sustainable Home: Practical projects, tips, and advice for maintaining a more eco-friendly household. Christine Liu provides practical advice on creating an eco-friendly household, emphasizing sustainability and its connection to personal well-being.

Your Brain on Nature: The Science of Nature's Influence on Your Health, Happiness and Vitality. Eva Selhub and

Alan Logan discuss the positive effects of nature on brain health and function, as well as overall well-being.

The Healthy Home: Simple Truths to Protect Your Family from Hidden Household Dangers. Dr. Myron Wentz and Dave Wentz delve into potential dangers in the home environment and provide insights into creating a healthier living space.

The Nature Fix: Why Nature Makes Us Happier, Healthier, and More Creative. Florence Williams explores the science behind why being in nature makes us feel good and promotes well-being.

Proactive Mental Health Building Block
Health Behavior

Health behavior refers to the day-to-day actions we take to enhance our well-being. This includes engagement in preventive medicine—such as regular screenings, vaccinations, and medical consultations—and adhering to a healthy lifestyle characterized by balanced nutrition, regular physical activity, adequate sleep, and avoiding risk factors like smoking and excessive alcohol consumption. The health behaviors that affect our physical health also play a significant role in our mental health. The following chapters address proactive mental health strategies related to health behavior. Staying current on preventive health care and maintaining a healthy lifestyle can have numerous mental health benefits:

Mental Health Benefits of Preventive Health Care

- **Reduced Anxiety:** Regular check-ups and screenings can alleviate the anxiety associated with uncertainty about one's health status. Knowing that you are taking steps to monitor and maintain your health can offer peace of mind.
- **Early Intervention:** Identifying mental health issues at an early stage through preventive care offers the opportunity for early intervention, which often leads to better outcomes.
- **Hormonal Balance:** Conditions like thyroid imbalances can significantly affect mental health. Preventive care can identify these issues before they manifest as mental health problems.
- **Reduced Risk of Depression:** Chronic illnesses can often lead to depression. Preventive healthcare can help in the early detection and management of chronic conditions, thereby reducing the risk of associated mental health problems.
- **Substance Abuse Prevention:** Regular health screenings may identify early signs of substance abuse, which has significant mental health implications. Early intervention can be vital.

Mental Health Benefits of a Healthy Lifestyle

- **Improved Mood:** Exercise releases endorphins, which are natural mood lifters. A balanced diet rich in essential nutrients can also positively affect neurotransmitter function, improving mood.
- **Stress Reduction:** Physical activity and relaxation techniques like meditation are proven to reduce stress levels.
- **Better Sleep:** Exercise and a balanced diet can significantly improve the quality of sleep, which is crucial for mental well-being.
- **Enhanced Cognitive Function:** A healthy lifestyle that includes regular physical activity, balanced nutrition, and adequate sleep can improve cognitive function, enhancing memory, attention, and problem-solving skills.
- **Increased Self-Esteem:** Taking active steps to improve physical health can lead to improved body image and self-esteem, which are important components of mental health.
- **Social Benefits:** Engaging in community sports or other social activities related to a healthy lifestyle can provide the additional benefit of social support, which is important for mental health.
- **Emotional Regulation:** Activities like yoga and meditation improve physical flexibility and strength and help in mindfulness training, which can improve emotional regulation and mental resilience.
- **Sense of Accomplishment:** Setting and achieving health goals, whether losing weight, running a mar-

athon, or quitting smoking, contributes to a sense of accomplishment and self-efficacy, which are positive mental health indicators.

How Culture Supports or Undermines Health Behavior

It is difficult to achieve healthy practices when cultural environments don't support them. In contrast, you are more likely to establish and maintain healthy behaviors in supportive cultural environments. Here are some ways in which culture impacts health behavior:

Supportive Aspects of Culture

- **Health Norms and Values:** People are more likely to engage in preventive care and healthy living practices in cultures that prioritize health.
- **Social Support:** A culture that values family and community will offer social support systems vital for maintaining good mental and physical health.
- **Traditional Practices:** Some cultures have traditional health practices, such as yoga or meditation, that may benefit well-being.
- **Information Sharing:** Cultures that value education and communication may offer better platforms for disseminating health information, thus enabling better health choices.
- **Healthy Rituals:** Some cultures have built-in rituals that promote health, like walking pilgrimages, dancing, or communal meals that are nutritionally balanced.

- **Stigma Reduction:** Open and inclusive cultures may have fewer stigmas surrounding mental health or medical conditions, encouraging people to seek help.

Undermining Aspects of Culture

- **Harmful Practices:** Some cultural practices, such as customs that discourage vaccinations or other preventive measures, can harm health.
- **Stigma and Taboos:** In some cultures, mental health struggles are stigmatized, which may discourage people from seeking help.
- **Misinformation:** In cultures where pseudoscience is prevalent or where there's distrust in medical professionals, people may be led astray from effective treatments and preventive measures.
- **Sedentary Lifestyle:** Modern culture, influenced by technology and convenience, often promotes sedentary behaviors that are detrimental to health.
- **Consumer Culture:** Promoting fast food, alcohol, and tobacco can contribute to unhealthy lifestyle choices.
- **Gender Norms:** In some cultures, gender norms may discourage people from engaging in certain healthy behaviors. For example, the idea that certain types of exercise or food are "masculine" or "feminine" can limit individuals' choices.
- **Socioeconomic Factors:** Cultural attitudes towards wealth and social status can indirectly affect health by dictating who has access to healthcare resources.

- **Fatalism:** In some cultures, believing that poor health outcomes are the result of fate or destiny can discourage people from seeking preventive healthcare and timely medical intervention.

Chapter 24

Benefit from Preventive Medicine

"The body hears everything your mind says."
— NAOMI JUDD

"Mental health is often missing from public health debates even though it's critical to well-being."
— DIANE ABBOTT

KEEPING UP WITH primary healthcare appointments is often stressful. It can be costly, inconvenient, time-consuming, and confusing. Many providers have packed schedules and lack the time or capacity to address mental health concerns. These constraints may lead to overprescribing mental health-related drugs and inadequate support for lifestyle remedies that might effectively address mental health concerns such as poor sleep, anxiety, and unhappiness.

Despite these flaws and drawbacks, working with a primary care provider who practices preventive medicine can be important to proactive mental health. Preventive medicine emphasizes the prevention of diseases and conditions before they develop or progress. Mental health issues, such as depression and anxiety, can adversely affect physical health and vice versa. It is crucial to address both aspects of health comprehensively.

Preventive medicine screenings, such as routine check-ups, vaccinations, and screenings for conditions like cancer, cardiovascular disease, and diabetes, play a significant role in maintaining overall health. These screenings can help detect potential physical and mental health problems early, allowing for timely intervention and treatment. If an illness goes undetected or untreated, it may increase stress, anxiety, or depression. Chronic physical health problems can interfere with daily functioning and diminish overall quality of life, contributing to mental health difficulties.

Benefits of Staying Current with Preventive Medicine

Here are some potential mental health benefits of preventive medicine:

- **Reduced Anxiety and Worry:** Regular preventive care, including screenings and check-ups, can help detect health problems early or provide reassurance of good health. This proactive approach can alleviate anxiety and worry associated with undiagnosed or untreated physical health concerns, allowing people to focus more on their mental well-being.

- **Improved Sense of Control:** When people take steps to maintain their physical health, such as adhering to recommended screenings and vaccinations, it can foster a sense of control, self-care, and empowerment.

- **Healthier Lifestyle Practices:** Preventive care often recommends positive health behaviors, such as regular exercise, proper nutrition, and adequate sleep. These behaviors are not only beneficial for physical health but also have a positive impact on mental health. Regular physical activity, for example, is associated with reduced symptoms of depression and anxiety and improved stress management.

- **Increased Resilience:** Being current on preventive medicine screenings and care can enhance an individual's resilience in the face of physical health challenges. By proactively addressing and managing physical health conditions, people may develop a sense of resilience and adaptive coping strategies that can extend to their mental health, enabling them to navigate life stressors better.

- **Medical Remedies for Illnesses:** Preventive care screenings may identify potential risk factors or early signs of illnesses that undermine mental health. Timely detection allows for early intervention and treatment, which can mitigate the impact of these conditions on mental health. In addition, medical providers may prescribe medicines that address anxiety, sleep disorders, and other mental health challenges.

Myths and Misunderstandings about Preventive Medicine

Several myths and misunderstandings about the relationship between mental health and preventive medicine can undermine well-being. Here are a few examples:

Myth: Mental health and physical health are unrelated.

Reality: Mental health and physical health are interconnected. Numerous studies have shown the bidirectional relationship between mental and physical well-being. Neglecting preventive medicine screenings and care can adversely affect mental health and vice versa.

Myth: Preventive care is only important for physical health.

Reality: Preventive care encompasses both physical and mental health. Regular screenings and preventive care can help detect and address physical health conditions early, reducing the potential negative impact on mental health. It also contributes to adopting positive health behaviors that benefit mental well-being.

Myth: Mental health issues cannot be improved through preventive care.

Reality: Preventive care can play a role in promoting mental health. By addressing physical health needs and engaging in positive health behaviors, people may experience improved overall well-being, positively influencing their mental health outcomes.

Myth: Mental health concerns are solely the responsibility of mental health professionals.

Reality: Although mental health professionals play a crucial role, addressing mental health concerns requires a collaborative approach. Primary care providers can integrate mental health screenings into routine care and provide appropriate referrals. Collaborative care models involving mental health and primary care professionals have shown positive outcomes.

Myth: Being current on preventive care eliminates the risk of mental health disorders.

Reality: Although preventive care is important, it does not guarantee immunity from mental health challenges. Some mental health conditions have complex causes that go beyond physical health factors. However, being current on preventive care can contribute to overall well-being and potentially reduce the risk or severity of certain mental health issues.

Myth: Access to preventive care is equal for everyone.

Reality: You or someone you know may be excluded from accessing preventive care due to socioeconomic factors, such as income, education, and insurance coverage. Demand access. Unchecked, these disparities can disproportionately affect marginalized populations, potentially leading to gaps in preventive care and subsequent impacts on mental health.

Preventive Medicine Self-Assessment

Preventive medicine recommendations are based on your health profile, age, gender, and risk factors. The following questions can help you assess your current efforts to practice preventative medicine:

1. Have I had a comprehensive check-up or wellness visit within the recommended timeframe?
2. Am I current on screenings such as blood pressure measurement, cholesterol level testing, or diabetes screening?
3. Have I received age-appropriate cancer screenings, such as mammograms, Pap smears, or colonoscopies?
4. Have I received all recommended vaccinations?
5. Have I received any recommended booster shots for vaccines I received earlier in life?
6. Have I undergone any mental health screenings or assessments, such as for depression, anxiety, or substance abuse?
7. Have I discussed my mental health concerns or symptoms with a healthcare provider?
8. Do I have any chronic medical conditions, and am I receiving regular follow-up care and screenings related to these conditions?
9. Am I adhering to the recommended guidelines for managing chronic conditions, such as regular blood tests, medication reviews, or lifestyle modifications?
10. Have I discussed preventive behaviors with my healthcare provider, such as tobacco cessation, weight management, or stress reduction strategies?
11. Am I following any personalized recommendations or action plans provided by my healthcare provider?

Finding a Preventive Medicine Provider

Finding a primary care provider who emphasizes preventive medicine can lead to a long-term health partnership focused on maintaining wellness and avoiding illness. Here are steps and tips to help you identify such a provider:

Do Your Research

- Organizations like the American College of Preventive Medicine or the American Board of Preventive Medicine have membership lists.
- Look for board certification in preventive medicine or family medicine. Some providers also have additional nutrition, fitness, or preventative health training.
- Many physicians and medical groups offer websites detailing their care philosophy, services, patient testimonials, etc. Look for evidence that the practitioner or medical group is supportive, a good listener, and interested in clients' mental well-being.
- Although they're not all accurate, patient reviews can provide insights into other patients' experiences and satisfaction levels.

Ask for Recommendations

- Ask friends, family, colleagues, and current medical care providers if they can recommend a provider who focuses on preventive care.

Interview Potential Primary Care Providers

Schedule a new patient visit or a meet-and-greet to determine whether you will be comfortable working with the provider. Ask about:

- Their philosophy on preventive medicine and patient education.
- Their availability for routine check-ups and screenings.
- Their stance on vaccines, alternative therapies, and nutrition.
- Weight loss programs, smoking cessation clinics, or other preventive-focused initiatives. These can be signs of their commitment to preventive care.

Check Your Compatibility

- Pay attention to the general atmosphere of the office. Are there educational materials about prevention? How friendly and helpful is the staff? Do you feel comfortable with the provider? The best primary care provider for you is skilled in preventive medicine and someone with whom you feel comfortable discussing your health concerns. It's crucial to trust and feel at ease with your provider, as open communication is a vital component of effective preventive care.

Optimizing Your Role in Preventive Medicine

Preventive medicine is a partnership between you and your healthcare providers so that you will be better positioned to prevent potential health issues, detect problems early, and maintain your well-being for the long term. Here's how you can help achieve preventive medicine:

- **Stay Informed:** Regularly educate yourself about recommended health screenings, vaccinations, and guidelines for your age, gender, and risk factors. New research and guidelines emerge frequently. Stay connected with reputable health organizations or websites. This knowledge helps you take proactive measures.

- **Schedule Regular Check-ups:** Have routine physical exams to monitor blood pressure, cholesterol levels, and other vital metrics. Undergo recommended screenings (e.g., mammograms, colonoscopies, prostate exams, bone density tests) based on age and risk. Have recommended dental care as well as routine eye and hearing exams.

- **Check Your Vaccinations:** Ensure you're current with recommended vaccines for your age and circumstances (e.g., flu shots, HPV, shingles, tetanus).

- **Manage Medications:** If on medications, ensure you take them as prescribed and review them with your healthcare provider regularly.

- **Keep Records:** Maintain a personal health record. This includes medical history, medications, allergies, immunizations, and significant health events.

- **Communicate:** Don't hesitate to see a healthcare professional if something feels off. Tell the professional if you did not achieve treatment recommendations or adopt healthy lifestyle changes.

- **Advocate for Yourself:** Be proactive in asking questions during medical appointments and seeking second opinions when needed.

Books on the Relationship Between Preventive Medicine and Mental Health

Several books and publications address this intersection between primary healthcare and mental health:

The Self-Care Solution: A Year of Becoming Happier, Healthier, and Fitter--One Month at a Time. Jennifer Ashton shares her year-long self-care journey, combining her personal experiences with medical insights.

The Empowered Patient: How to Get the Right Diagnosis, Buy the Cheapest Drugs, Beat Your Insurance Company, and Get the Best Medical Care Every Time. Elizabeth Cohen provides readers with practical advice on taking charge of their health and navigating the healthcare system.

How to Be a Patient: The Essential Guide to Navigating the World of Modern Medicine. Sana Goldberg provides insights into how patients can take a proactive role in all aspects of their healthcare, including prevention.

Chapter 25

Get Help with Mental Health Problems Early On

"What mental health needs is more sunlight, more candor, and more unashamed conversation."
— GLENN CLOSE

"Despite the universal vulnerability of all persons to mental disorders, many countries allocate less than 1% of their health budget to mental health."
— WORLD HEALTH ORGANIZATION (WHO)

GETTING HELP WITH mental health problems early on means seeking assistance, treatment, or intervention during the initial stages of the issue or disorder, often before it becomes more severe or chronic. Early intervention in health issues emphasizes proactive rather than reactive care, addressing issues at their onset rather than waiting for them to become severe.

There's a significant gap between the onset of mental health symptoms and when people seek professional help. This delay, often called the "treatment gap," exists for various reasons. According to research findings, people often experience symptoms for several years before seeking help. For example, it's estimated that people with anxiety disorders wait, on average, 11 years after symptom onset before receiving treatment.

Globally, the World Health Organization (WHO) estimates that approximately two-thirds of people with a known mental health challenge never seek help from a health professional. Below are some of the factors that contribute to this treatment gap:

- **Stigma:** One of the most significant barriers to early intervention in mental health is the social stigma attached to mental illnesses. People often fear judgment or discrimination if they openly seek help for mental health concerns.
- **Lack of Awareness:** Many people, as well as those around them, may not recognize the early signs of mental health challenges or may not take them seriously, attributing them to phases, moods, or temporary circumstances.
- **Access to Care:** Mental health services are not readily available or affordable in many places, making it challenging for people to seek help even when they recognize the need. The cost of mental health treatment can be prohibitive for many, especially in countries without universal healthcare.

- **Misinformation:** False or misleading mental health information can also delay treatment. Some people may believe they can "snap out of it" or that treatment is ineffective.
- **Cultural Factors:** In some cultures, mental health challenges are not recognized as medical conditions and may be attributed to moral failings or lack of willpower. This can deter people from seeking help.

The Benefits of Getting Treatment Early

Getting help early on refers to identifying, addressing, and intervening in mental health challenges before they become more severe or deeply entrenched. Seeking early help is crucial for various reasons:

- **Prevention of Severity:** Mental health issues can escalate if not addressed. Early intervention can prevent conditions from worsening, which might otherwise lead to more severe complications, including self-harm, substance abuse, or even suicide.
- **Reduced Duration of Treatment:** Addressing mental health issues early can often reduce the overall duration of treatment, as less entrenched problems may require shorter therapeutic intervention.
- **Cost-Effectiveness:** Early intervention can be more cost-effective in the long run. Addressing an issue before it becomes severe can prevent the need for more intensive and costly treatments later. Early intervention also reduces disruptions to employment.
- **Improved Life Quality:** Identifying and addressing mental health problems early can help people maintain

relationships, continue their education or work, and participate more fully in their communities.

- **Stigma Reduction:** Addressing mental health issues promptly and openly can help reduce the stigma surrounding them. As more people talk about and seek early help, mental health can become a more normalized topic of discussion.

- **Better Coping Strategies:** Early intervention often involves equipping people with coping mechanisms and strategies that can be valuable throughout their lives. This early skill-building can help them navigate future challenges more effectively.

- **Support Systems:** Getting help early often involves creating or leveraging support systems, be it through therapy, support groups, or family and friends. Delays may diminish support and frustrate those willing to help.

Myths and Misunderstandings about Getting Early Help with Mental Health

There are several myths and misconceptions about getting help with mental health that could, if unchallenged, undermine your timely help-seeking behaviors.

Myth: I should wait and see if the problem goes away.

Reality: Although some mental and physical health issues may resolve spontaneously, many conditions benefit from early intervention. Waiting too long before seeking help can lead to worsening symptoms, increased distress, and a potentially more challenging treatment process. It's best to consult with healthcare professionals who can assess your situation and provide appropriate guidance.

Myth: I missed my chance at early intervention because I've been living with this problem for a long time.

Reality: Even if you've been struggling for weeks, months, or years, you're still better off getting help now than letting the situation persist. Now is better than later or never.

Myth: Early intervention is only necessary for severe or chronic conditions.

Reality: Early intervention is essential for various mental and physical health concerns, regardless of severity or chronicity. Addressing problems at their early stages can prevent them from escalating or becoming chronic in the first place. Prompt intervention is beneficial for mild and severe conditions, as it can minimize distress, improve outcomes, and reduce long-term impact.

Myth: Getting help early means I'm weak or incapable of handling my problems.

Reality: Seeking help early is a sign of strength and self-awareness. Recognizing the need for assistance and taking proactive steps to address mental and physical health concerns demonstrates resilience and a commitment to personal well-being. It's important to remember that seeking help is a courageous and wise choice, allowing you to gain support and acquire effective strategies to manage your challenges.

Myth: Early intervention is only for people with diagnosed conditions.

Reality: Early intervention is not limited to diagnosed conditions alone. It can also benefit people experiencing early signs, symptoms, or risk factors associated with mental health problems. Identifying and addressing these early warning signs can help prevent the progression of difficulties and promote overall well-being.

Myth: I can handle it independently or rely solely on self-help resources.

Reality: Although self-help resources can be valuable, they may not always be sufficient for addressing complex mental health issues. Seeking professional help early provides access to specialized knowledge, evidence-based treatments, and tailored support. Mental health professionals are trained to provide appropriate guidance, interventions, and resources for your needs.

Self-Assessment for Early Action on Mental Health

Determining if you're getting help with mental health issues early on involves self-awareness, reflection, and perhaps professional guidance. Here are some questions you might consider:

1. Have I noticed changes in my mood, thoughts, or behavior recently?
2. Am I experiencing symptoms that interfere with my daily life, relationships, or work?
3. Have my friends, family, or coworkers expressed concern about changes they've noticed in me?
4. Am I avoiding seeking help due to self-imposed or societal stigma?
5. Am I aware of the potential risks if I delay treatment for my condition?
6. Do I have access to the mental healthcare I need?
7. Have I consulted a healthcare professional about my symptoms?
8. Am I actively participating in my treatment?
9. Do I have a preliminary or formal diagnosis from a qualified mental health professional?
10. Have I started any treatment, such as medication or therapy?
11. Does my treatment plan align with early intervention best practices for my condition?
12. Do I have a support network (family, friends, professionals) to help me through early treatment?

Improving Your Ability to Act Early

Improving your capacity to act early involves a multifaceted approach that includes education, lifestyle changes, and support from healthcare professionals and loved ones. Make it a regular practice to check in on your mental health and proactively seek help when needed. Here are some strategies for recognizing and acting upon mental health challenges early:

- See current information from credible sources to educate yourself about the early symptoms of various mental health conditions. The more you know, the better you'll identify problems early.
- Discuss mental health openly with trusted family and friends to create an environment where sharing concerns is easier. Sometimes, others notice changes in your behavior before you do. Invite them to share their observations.
- Establish a relationship with a mental healthcare provider for regular check-ups, and don't hesitate to consult them when you notice symptoms. Make it a habit to assess your mental health periodically as you would your physical health.
- Make use of online mental health screenings from credible sources. Although not a substitute for professional diagnosis, they can be a wake-up call to seek further help.
- Track declines in self-care (i.e., eating well, exercising, and getting enough sleep). Declines in these areas may be early warning signals that your mental health needs attention.
- Practice mindfulness and stress management techniques. These can help you become more aware of your emotional state.
- Use mental health apps that track mood and symptoms. They can provide valuable data and trends over time.

- Familiarize yourself with what mental health services your insurance covers.
- Educate yourself and others to challenge stigmatizing beliefs about mental health. The more openly mental health is discussed, the less stigma is attached to it, making it easier for people to seek help early.
- Keep a list of emergency contacts, hotlines, and mental healthcare providers readily available.
- Have a plan of what steps to take if you notice significant symptoms, including who to call and where to go.
- Be kind to yourself. Acknowledging that you need help is a brave step. Be compassionate toward yourself as you navigate the early stages of seeking help.

Books About Early Mental Health Intervention

Here are books about why, when, and how to address mental health challenges.

Early Intervention in Psychiatry: EI of Nearly Everything for Better Mental Health. This book, edited by Peter Byrne and Alan Rosen, discusses the importance of early intervention (EI) in various psychiatric conditions.

Lost Connections: Uncovering the Real Causes of Depression–and the Unexpected Solutions. Johann Hari explores various factors contributing to depression and emphasizes the importance of early interventions.

The Whole-Brain Child. Daniel Siegel and Tina Payne Bryson offer strategies for nurturing children's mental well-being, emphasizing early intervention and understanding the developing brain.

Chapter 26

Eat Well

"Eat like you love yourself. Move like you love yourself. Speak like you love yourself. Act like you love yourself."

— TARA STILES

"The shared meal elevates eating from a mechanical process of fueling the body to a ritual of family and community, from the mere animal biology to an act of culture."

— MICHAEL POLLAN

DIET PLAYS A major role in mental well-being. Early civilizations, such as the Greeks and Romans, recognized the connection between diet and mental well-being. Philosophers like Hippocrates emphasized the role of diet in maintaining overall health, including mental health. In the 19th century, researchers began investigating the effects of specific nutrients on mental health. For example, the discovery of pellagra, a niacin deficiency disease that can lead to mental symptoms., The 20th century saw significant advancements in our understanding of vitamins and their role in mental health. For example, it was discovered that thiamine (vitamin B1) was needed to help cure beriberi, which affects both physical and mental health. In recent decades, scientific research has expanded our understanding of how specific nutrients and dietary patterns impact mental health. Studies have explored the effects of nutritional components on conditions like depression, anxiety, and cognitive decline. The relationship between healthy eating and mental health is an increasingly important area of study in psychology, neuroscience, and nutrition. Here are some key findings to consider:

Physiological Mechanisms

- **Nutrient Intake:** Certain nutrients like omega-3 fatty acids in fatty fish and other foods are linked to better mental health outcomes. These nutrients are believed to facilitate better brain function and may help alleviate symptoms of depression and anxiety.
- **Gut-Brain Axis:** The gut is often called the "second brain" because it produces many of the same neurotransmitters found in the brain. Foods that promote a healthy gut microbiome (like probiotics and fiber-rich foods) can influence mental well-being.
- **Blood Sugar Levels:** Foods high in sugar and refined carbohydrates can cause fluctuations in blood sugar levels, leading to mood swings and irritability.

- **Hormonal Balance:** Some foods can impact the hormonal balance in the body, affecting mental health. For instance, foods rich in antioxidants can help manage stress by reducing cortisol, a stress hormone.

Psychological Aspects

- **Mood and Emotions:** Consuming nutrient-rich foods can elevate mood and combat depression and anxiety. Conversely, foods high in sugar and fat can contribute to feelings of lethargy and low mood.
- **Cognitive Function:** Adequate nutrition is critical for cognitive function, including memory, problem-solving, and critical thinking. Deficiencies in certain nutrients can lead to decreased cognitive function, impacting mental health.
- **Body Image:** Healthy eating contributes to better body image and self-esteem, key components of mental well-being. Unhealthy eating patterns can contribute to poor body image and low self-esteem, creating a cycle that affects mental health.
- **Mindfulness:** Consciously making healthier food choices can be seen as a form of self-care, promoting mental well-being.

Sociocultural Factors

- **Cultural Norms:** Different cultures have different norms around eating, and what is considered 'healthy' can vary. However, the core principles of nutrition apply universally and can be adapted to fit various cultural preferences.

- **Social Eating:** In many cultures, eating is a social activity. Engaging in healthy eating habits within a community can promote mental well-being through social interaction and the release of feel-good hormones like oxytocin.

- **Access and Equity:** Unfortunately, access to healthy food can be limited in certain communities, contributing to poor mental health outcomes. The high cost and inaccessibility of healthy foods in low-income communities can undermine good nutrition.

Healthy Eating and Positive Body Image Are Mental Health Indicators

Unhealthy eating can be associated with an unfavorable view of our bodies. Poor body image refers to a negative perception of one's body, often involving a distorted view of one's shape, size, or physical attributes. This negative self-perception can lead to emotional distress, low self-esteem, and harmful behaviors aimed at changing one's body, such as extreme dieting, excessive exercise, or disordered eating.

Issues around body image can significantly impact an individual's mental well-being and contribute to or exacerbate various forms of mental health challenges. Several mental health challenges are associated with poor body image:

- Eating Disorders like anorexia nervosa, bulimia nervosa, and binge-eating disorder are strongly associated with body image concerns.

- Body Dysmorphic Disorder (BDD) is a mental health condition where a person obsesses over perceived flaws in their appearance, which are often minor or not observable to others.
- Poor body image can contribute to depressive and anxious symptoms; conversely, these conditions can negatively affect one's body image.
- Self-worth is often tied to body image; a negative body image can result in diminished self-esteem.
- Concerns about body image can exacerbate social anxiety and lead to avoidance of social situations, further impacting mental health.

The Mental Health Benefits of Healthy Eating

Numerous mental health benefits are associated with eating a nutritious diet. Here are some notable benefits:

- **Reduced risk of depression:** Diets rich in fruits, vegetables, whole grains, lean proteins, and omega-3 fatty acids have been linked to a decreased likelihood of depressive symptoms. On the other hand, diets high in processed foods, refined sugars, and unhealthy fats have been associated with an increased risk of depression.
- **Improved mood and emotional well-being:** Nutrient-dense foods, such as fruits, vegetables, whole grains, and lean proteins, provide essential vitamins, minerals, and antioxidants that support brain health and neurotransmitter function. These nutrients are vital in regulating mood and emotions, potentially

leading to greater emotional resilience and well-being.

- **Enhanced cognitive function:** A healthy diet has been associated with better cognitive function, including improved memory, attention, and concentration. Nutrients like omega-3 fatty acids, B vitamins, antioxidants, and phytochemicals in whole foods support brain health and promote optimal cognitive performance. Conversely, diets high in saturated fats, added sugars, and processed foods have been linked to cognitive decline and increased risk of neurodegenerative disorders.

- **Reduced anxiety and stress:** Certain nutrients have been shown to have anxiety-reducing effects. For example, omega-3 fatty acids found in fatty fish, walnuts, and flaxseeds have been associated with a lower risk of anxiety disorders. Additionally, diets rich in fruits and vegetables, which are high in antioxidants and phytochemicals, have been linked to reduced stress levels and improved overall mental resilience.

- **Enhanced physical health:** Maintaining a healthy diet supports physical health, positively influencing mental health. A balanced diet helps regulate energy levels, promotes better sleep patterns, and provides the necessary nutrients for optimal brain functioning. Feeling physically healthy and nourished often translates into improved mental health and greater well-being.

Myths and Misunderstandings about Healthy Eating and Mental Health

Several myths and misunderstandings exist about the relationship between mental health and eating a healthy diet. Here are a few to consider:

Myth: Only specific diets, like the Mediterranean diet, are effective for mental health.

Reality: Although certain dietary patterns, such as the Mediterranean diet, have been extensively studied and shown to be beneficial for mental health, there is no one-size-fits-all diet that guarantees positive outcomes. People have diverse nutritional needs, and the impact of diet on mental health can vary across individuals. Focus on overall dietary quality, including various whole foods, rather than solely on a specific diet.

Myth: Eating a healthy diet means restricting all "unhealthy" foods.

Reality: Adopting a healthy diet does not necessitate eliminating all "unhealthy" foods. Perfectionistic thinking around food can lead to disordered eating patterns or an unhealthy relationship with food. Aiming for a balanced approach that incorporates a wide range of nutrient-dense foods while allowing for occasional indulgences is important. Flexibility and moderation are key to maintaining a healthy relationship with food and mental well-being.

Myth: Everyone's mental health can be improved by changing their diet.

Reality: Mental health is influenced by a multitude of factors, including genetics, environment, life experiences, and social support, in addition to diet. Although a healthy diet can contribute to improved mental well-being, it cannot single-handedly address all aspects of mental health. A holistic approach, considering various factors and tailored to each person's needs, is crucial for mental health.

Healthy Eating Self-Assessment

The following questions can help you reflect on your current dietary habits and their potential impact on your mental well-being.

1. How does my diet make me feel physically and mentally? Do I experience sustained energy throughout the day or frequent energy crashes? Do I notice any changes in my mood, concentration, or cognitive function after certain meals or food choices?

2. Am I consuming a variety of nutrient-dense foods? Do my meals include a wide range of fruits, vegetables, whole grains, lean proteins, and healthy fats? Am I incorporating sources of omega-3 fatty acids into my diet, such as fatty fish, flaxseeds, or walnuts?

3. Am I eating a limited amount of (or no) processed foods, sugary snacks, or sweet beverages? Am I aware of the potential impact of these foods on my mental well-being, such as mood fluctuations or energy dips?

4. Am I adequately hydrated? Do I drink enough water throughout the day? Do I notice any cognitive or mood changes when I am adequately hydrated versus when I am not?

5. Am I listening to my body's hunger and fullness cues? Am I eating mindfully and paying attention to my body's signals of hunger and satiety? Am I engaging in emotional or stress-related eating patterns?

6. Have I noticed any specific food sensitivities or intolerances that affect my mental well-being? Do certain foods or ingredients make me feel bloated and tired or affect my mood negatively?

7. Do I have a balanced approach to my diet? Do I enjoy occasional treats while focusing on nourishing my body with nutrient-rich foods? Am I practicing moderation and avoiding strict or restrictive eating patterns?

8. Have I identified ways to both enjoy cultural traditions such as holiday meals and maintain a healthy diet?

9. Am I balancing addressing my mental health needs and enjoying my relationship with food?

10. Do I take advantage of opportunities to eat with others?

Improving Your Capacity for Healthy Eating

Changing your diet can be difficult, notably when societal norms do not support your health goals. Changing your diet to improve mental health is a multi-step process. Here are some suggestions for going about it:

- **Gain Support:** Share your goals and your journey with supportive friends or family. They can offer moral support, accountability, and even join you in making healthier choices.
- **Identify Triggers and Patterns:** Keep a food and mood journal for a week or two to identify emotional triggers and times you tend to eat unhealthily. Note your mood before and after eating.
- **Incorporate Physical Exercise:** Exercise is another excellent way to boost mental health and often assists healthy eating.
- **Set Your Goals:** Take a close look at your diet to identify gaps or areas for improvement.
- **Plan Meals:** Meals incorporating foods rich in essential nutrients boost mental health. Make a shopping list based on this.
- **Shop:** Stick to your list when shopping and try to shop the perimeter of the store, where fresh produce is usually located.
- **Prepare Meals:** Take time out to prepare meals. This minimizes the temptation to go for quick, unhealthy options.
- **Eat with Intention:** Practice eating without distractions and savor each bite.
- **Track and Celebrate Progress:** Record your meals and moods to track how your new diet affects your mental health. This can help you make necessary adjustments.

Books About Mental Health and Healthy Eating

Books on the intersection of mental health and healthy eating can provide valuable insights into how dietary choices impact emotional and psychological states. Here are some books on the topic:

Intuitive Eating: A Revolutionary Program That Works. Evelyn Tribole and Elyse Resch deal with the emotional aspects of eating and encourage a balanced and mindful approach to food.

The Happiness Diet: A Nutritional Prescription for a Sharp Brain, Balanced Mood, and Lean, Energized Body. Tyler Graham and Drew Ramsey dive deep into how modern diets can impact brain health and mood disorders.

How to Eat. Thich Nhat Hanh and Dr. Lilian Cheung combine mindfulness practices with healthy eating habits, helping you eat in a manner that supports mental and physical well-being.

Nutrient Power: Heal Your Biochemistry and Heal Your Brain. William Walsh discusses various nutrient-based treatments that can help improve mental health conditions.

Genius Foods: Become Smarter, Happier, and More Productive While Protecting Your Brain for Life. Max Lugavere and Paul Grewal provide information on how certain foods can improve brain function.

The Anti-Anxiety Diet: A Whole Body Program to Stop Racing Thoughts, Banish Worry and Live Panic-Free. Ali Miller focuses on how diet can impact anxiety levels and provides practical tips for change.

Brain Food: The Surprising Science of Eating for Cognitive Power. Lisa Mosconi explores the link between cognitive functioning and nutrition.

Eat Complete: The 21 Nutrients That Fuel Brainpower, Boost Weight Loss, and Transform Your Health. Drew Ramsey outlines specific nutrients for mental health and where to find them in food.

The Mood Cure: The 4-Step Program to Take Charge of Your Emotions—Today. Julia Ross outlines how different amino acids, nutrients, and dietary changes can help treat mood disorders.

Chapter 27

Avoid Addictions

"Addiction is a family disease. One person may use, but the whole family suffers."

— SHELLY LEWIS

"Your best days are ahead of you. The movie starts when the guy gets sober and puts his life back together; it doesn't end there."

— BUCKY SINISTER

ONE MENTAL HEALTH goal is to enjoy life without dependencies that rob freedoms, happiness, and success. In this chapter, the focus will be on the overuse of drugs like alcohol and narcotics, many behaviors can become addictive including sex, exercise, and work. It is important to recognize when the need for something undermines your ability to set limits. It is also important to develop skills and seek support for addressing such potential dependencies. When a behavior such as alcohol or other drug use leads to negative consequences in a person's life—such as health problems, difficulties in relationships, or legal issues—it is often categorized as abuse. Dependence or addiction occurs when the individual builds up a tolerance to a substance or activity and experiences withdrawal symptoms without it.

The line between use and abuse can be hard to identify, and the shift from use to abuse can be hard to predict. What might be moderate use for one person could have adverse effects on another. Individuals can (and often do) experience a shift from use to abuse. Others may consume in moderation without experiencing significant negative effects on their mental health.

Substance Use Disorder (SUD)

Substance use disorder (SUD), formerly known as substance abuse or addiction, is a complex and chronic medical condition characterized by the problematic and compulsive use of one or more substances, such as alcohol, drugs (including prescription medications), or other substances, despite harmful consequences. These substances are typically used for recreational, social, or ceremonial purposes, although they can also be used medically or therapeutically in some instances. They are classified in various ways:

- Stimulants, such as caffeine, nicotine, amphetamines, and cocaine, stimulate the central nervous system, making the person feel more awake, alert, or energetic.

- Depressants, such as alcohol, benzodiazepines, and certain sleep medications, slow down central nervous system activity, often making the person feel relaxed, less anxious, or sleepy.
- Hallucinogens, such as LSD, psilocybin, and DMT, alter perception, thoughts, and feelings, leading to hallucinations or altered states of consciousness.
- Opioids, such as heroin, morphine, and prescription pain medications, primarily affect the nervous system to reduce pain, but they also have a high potential for addiction and abuse.
- Psychoactive cannabinoids, such as the THC found in marijuana, are used for their psychoactive and physiological effects, including euphoria, increased appetite, and relaxation.
- Alcohol is an organic compound that depresses the central nervous system, leading to changes in behavior, mood, and mental state. It is commonly consumed in social settings and has various cultural and religious significance.

Alcohol and recreational drugs can undermine mental health by, for example, disrupting brain chemistry. Substance use can impair judgment, increase impulsivity, and exacerbate symptoms of anxiety and depression. Prolonged or heavy substance use may induce substance-induced psychosis, mood disorders, or cognitive impairments. Long-term abuse often results in multiple physical illnesses that undermine brain health.

The Benefits of Avoiding the Abuse of Alcohol and Other Drugs

Although moderate consumption of certain substances might have some perceived advantages, abuse or excessive use can harm mental health. Here are some of the mental health benefits of abstaining or minimizing use:

- **Better Decision-Making:** Substance abuse can cloud judgment and hinder the ability to make rational decisions. Avoiding such abuse improves decision-making capabilities.
- **Enhanced Memory:** Alcohol and drug abuse can negatively impact short-term and long-term memory. Abstaining helps preserve cognitive function.
- **Mood Stability:** Substance abuse is often linked with mood swings, irritability, and emotional instability. Abstinence can lead to improved mood regulation.
- **Reduced Anxiety:** Although some substances might temporarily relieve anxiety, their abuse often increases anxiety levels or even panic attacks over time.
- **Prevention of Depression:** Alcohol and certain drugs are depressants, and their abuse can lead to long-term depressive symptoms.
- **Improved Relationships:** Substance abuse can strain relationships due to erratic or violent behavior, neglect, or other types of emotional abuse. Abstinence can foster healthier relationships.
- **Better Social Interactions:** People are encouraged to develop better social skills without the crutch of substances.

- **Increased Self-Esteem:** Substance abuse can lead to feelings of guilt, shame, and low self-worth. Abstaining helps improve self-esteem and confidence.
- **Sense of Accomplishment:** Avoiding abuse can provide a significant emotional and psychological boost, creating a sense of empowerment and accomplishment.
- **Reduced Risk of Mental Health Challenges:** Substance abuse is often linked with a higher risk of developing mental health challenges like depression, anxiety disorders, and even more severe conditions like psychosis.
- **Enhanced Coping Strategies:** When they don't rely on substances as a coping mechanism, people are more likely to seek healthier methods of stress management, which have a more positive impact on mental health.

Myths and Misunderstandings about SUD

Several myths or misunderstandings surround the relationship between mental health and SUD.

Myth: Substance use is an effective way to cope with mental health problems.

Reality: Many individuals may turn to substances to cope with symptoms of mental health issues. However, substances provide only temporary relief and can worsen mental health conditions in the long run. Developing healthy coping strategies, seeking professional help, and building a solid support network are more effective ways to manage mental health challenges.

Myth: Everyone can self-regulate substance use without consequences.

Reality: The effects of substance use can vary significantly among individuals due to factors such as genetics, underlying mental health conditions, and personal vulnerabilities. What may be considered moderate use for one person could still have negative consequences for another. In addition, some substances are more addictive than others.

Myth: Prescription drugs are safe.

Reality: Prescription medications like opioids, sedatives, and stimulants are potentially addictive and dangerous, in some cases more so than illicit drugs.

Myth: SUD is primarily a youth issue.

Reality: Substance abuse can affect people of all ages, including older adults, who are often overlooked in this context.

Myth: Addicts are bad or weak people.

Reality: Addiction is a health condition, not a moral failing. Stigmatizing attitudes toward addiction can discourage people from seeking help.

Myth: You have to hit rock bottom to seek help.

Reality: Early intervention often leads to better outcomes. Recovery is possible at any stage. Waiting for a "low point" could result in unnecessary suffering and danger. Although earlier intervention is preferable, seeking help and making a positive change is never too late.

Myth: Willpower is enough to quit.

Reality: Willpower alone is rarely enough to help a person overcome SUD and stay sober. Addiction is a complex interplay of biological, psychological, and environmental factors. Professional help is often necessary.

Myth: Detox alone is sufficient treatment.

Reality: Although detox helps remove the substance from the system, it doesn't address the underlying issues leading to substance abuse.

Myth: One treatment approach fits all.

Reality: Treatment must be individualized, considering the specific substance(s), underlying mental health conditions, and other personal factors.

Myth: Relapse equals failure.

Reality: Recovery is a process that often includes setbacks. A relapse isn't a sign of failure but a cue for readjusting treatment strategies.

Self-Assessment for SUD

A thorough assessment for SUD often involves a combination of standardized questionnaires, clinical interviews, and a comprehensive evaluation of an individual's history and current situation. If you drink alcohol or use other drugs, answers to the following questions may help you recognize possible use issues:

1. **Loss of Control:** Have you ever tried to cut down or control your substance use but found it difficult or impossible to do so?

2. **Cravings:** Do you experience strong cravings or urges to use the substance?

3. **Negative Consequences:** Have you continued to use the substance even when it has caused or worsened physical or psychological problems or led to social or interpersonal difficulties?

4. **Time Spent:** How much time do you spend obtaining, using, or recovering from the effects of the substance?

5. **Neglected Activities:** Have you given up or reduced important social, occupational, or recreational activities because of substance use?

6. **Tolerance:** Have you needed to use more of the substance over time to achieve the desired effect, or have you noticed reduced effects when using the same amount?

7. **Withdrawal:** Have you experienced withdrawal symptoms when you stopped using the substance, or have you used the substance to relieve or avoid withdrawal symptoms?

8. **Unsuccessful Attempts to Quit:** Have you made repeated unsuccessful efforts to control, cut down, or quit using the substance?

9. **Loss of Interest:** Have you lost interest in or reduced participation in activities that were once important to you because of substance use?

10. **Continued Use Despite Knowledge of Harm:** Have you continued to use the substance even when you knew it was causing or worsening a physical or psychological problem?

A diagnosis of SUD is typically made when an individual meets at least two of these criteria within a 12-month period.

Addressing SUD

SUD is multifaceted. The best solutions often require multiple approaches. Addressing SUD often takes time and persistence over multiple attempts. The following strategies often help:

- Early identification through screening in primary care settings can help you better assess your needs.
- Equip yourself with knowledge about SUD. Consider the books listed at the end of this chapter.
- Find or create supportive physical and social environments. Avoid groups and environments that are likely to trigger SUD. Spend your time in subcultures with strong norms for avoiding SUD-related substances or behaviors. Surround yourself with groups and settings that have a strong sense of community.

- Consider Cognitive Behavioral Therapy (CBT), Motivational Interviewing (MI), and other evidence-based therapies for treating SUD.
- Antidepressants and anti-anxiety medications can sometimes be prescribed to treat underlying mental health conditions that are associated with drug abuse.
- Programs like AA (Alcoholics Anonymous) or SMART Recovery can offer peer support for recovery.
- Substance abuse often affects not just the individual but the entire family. Family therapy and Al-Anon can be helpful.

Books on SUD

Books on addiction address the impact on society, how to recognize addiction, the physiological and psychological processes of addiction, and how to overcome addiction. Here are some of the books on this important subject.

Sober for Good: New Solutions for Drinking Problems--Advice from Those Who Have Succeeded. Anne Fletcher shares accounts from people who have successfully quit drinking, providing diverse strategies for sobriety.

High Price: A Neuroscientist's Journey of Self-Discovery That Challenges Everything You Know About Drugs and Society. Carl Hart explores the science of drug addiction and challenges societal perceptions about it.

The Recovery Book: Answers to All Your Questions About Addiction and Alcoholism and Finding Health and Happiness in Sobriety. Al Mooney, Catherine Dold, and Howard Eisenberg offer a comprehensive guide for people in all stages of recovery. Written by a doctor specializing in addiction medicine and veteran health writers, the book covers a wide range of topics. These include understanding the brain chemistry of addiction, the stages of recovery, and coping mechanisms. It also provides advice on managing relapses and maintaining a drug-free life, including aspects related to work, social life, and mental health. The book is designed to be accessible, offering real-world advice backed by medical expertise. It is a reliable manual for anyone touched by addiction, be it the person in recovery, family members, or even healthcare providers.

Clean: Overcoming Addiction and Ending America's Greatest Tragedy. David Sheff offers an impassioned plea to address addiction and end America's drug epidemic. This book explores addiction, why it starts, and how it can be treated. Sheff combines personal anecdotes with a review of the science and strategies behind prevention and treatment. He challenges stigmas and myths surrounding addiction, arguing that it should be treated as a preventable, treatable health issue rather than a moral failing. The book also offers individual and societal solutions, suggesting policy changes, treatment options, and educational reforms.

Love and Addiction. Stanton Peele and Archie Brodsky challenge the traditional medical models that treat addiction solely as a physiological condition, arguing that addiction is more than just a chemical dependency; it can manifest in relationships and other non-substance-related behaviors. The authors delve into how emotional dependencies can become destructive and argue that societal norms and expectations often contribute to these patterns. The book suggests more integrated, humanistic approaches to treating addiction.

Chapter 28

Rest Well

"Almost everything will work again if you unplug it for a few minutes, including you."

— ANNE LAMOTT

"If you get tired, learn to rest, not to quit."

— BANKSY

BEING "RESTED" CAN vary from person to person, but generally, it refers to physical and mental recovery or rejuvenation. When someone says they feel rested, they typically mean that they feel refreshed and ready to tackle tasks or challenges. Being well-rested is often the result of adequate sleep, but it can also involve mental relaxation and emotional calm. In a broader context, "being rested" refers to taking a break from routine or work, giving the mind and body time to recover and rejuvenate. This can include vacations, days off, or even short breaks during the day to meditate or relax.

Different forms of rest are crucial for maintaining well-being, enhancing productivity, and ensuring good mental health. Understanding the various types of rest can help you identify which ones you might be lacking and need to incorporate into your life for better overall wellness. Here are some forms of rest:

Physical Rest

- **Sleep:** The most obvious form of rest, vital for physical recovery and cognitive function.
- **Napping:** Short periods of sleep to recharge during the day.
- **Passive Rest:** Sitting quietly, deep breathing, and other low-energy activities.

Mental Rest

- **Mindfulness/Meditation:** Exercises to quiet the mind and focus attention.
- **Unplugging:** Taking breaks from electronic devices.
- **Daydreaming:** Letting your mind wander without a particular goal or focus.

Emotional Rest

- **Deep Conversations:** Sharing and unburdening feelings, thoughts, or stress with someone you trust.

- **Setting Boundaries:** Saying no when needed to manage your emotional and physical energy.
- **Self-Care Activities:** Engaging in activities that bring joy and relaxation.

Social Rest

- **Alone Time:** Time spent without others to recharge.
- **Quality Time:** Spending time with loved ones where you can be yourself.
- **Community Engagement:** Feeling a sense of belonging in a community can be a restful experience for some.

Spiritual Rest

- **Prayer/Reflection:** Taking time for spiritual or religious practices.
- **Nature Walks:** Engaging with nature can have a spiritual restorative effect.
- **Reading Philosophical/Spiritual Texts:** Some find solace and rest in intellectual or spiritual pursuits.

Creative Rest

- **Artistic Expression:** Painting, drawing, or other creative outlets can be rejuvenating.
- **Listening to Music:** For some, music provides a mental break and inspires them.
- **Hobbies:** Non-work activities that engage different parts of the brain.

Sensory Rest

- **Reducing Overstimulation:** Dimming lights, reducing noise, and minimizing strong smells.
- **Grounding Techniques:** Activities that bring focus back to the present, such as touching a piece of fabric or focusing on your breath.
- **Tactile Activities:** Simple activities like molding clay or cooking can offer sensory rest.

Sleep and Being Rested

Sleep quantity and quality are key elements of being rested. There is a strong bidirectional relationship between sleep and mental health. Poor sleep can contribute to developing and exacerbating mental health conditions, while mental health issues can disrupt sleep patterns.

Sleep quality refers to how well one sleeps rather than just the duration. Quality sleep is crucial for various aspects of health, including mental well-being, physical strength, and overall quality of life. Several components contribute to sleep quality:

- **Sleep Latency:** The time it takes to fall asleep. Typically, falling asleep within 15-20 minutes is considered good.
- **Sleep Duration:** Although not the sole indicator of sleep quality, the amount of sleep one gets is essential. For adults, 7-9 hours is generally recommended.
- **Sleep Efficiency:** This is the ratio of the total time spent asleep to the time spent in bed. Higher efficiency is better and is usually over 85%.

- **Sleep Architecture:** This refers to the pattern of sleep cycles, including REM (rapid eye movement) and non-REM stages. A typical night should include multiple cycles of transitioning through these stages.
- **Awakenings:** Fewer awakenings and the ability to go back to sleep quickly contribute to better sleep quality.
- **Restfulness:** How you feel upon waking up; quality sleep should leave you feeling refreshed and alert.

The Benefits of Being Rested

There are mental health benefits associated with getting adequate rest:

- **Emotional Regulation:** Adequate rest helps people manage their emotions effectively, reducing the risk of mood swings, irritability, and emotional reactivity. It promotes a more stable and balanced emotional state.
- **Improved Cognitive Function:** Getting enough rest supports optimal cognitive functioning. It enhances attention, concentration, and decision-making abilities, improving cognitive performance. Adequate sleep also aids memory consolidation, making retaining and recalling information easier.
- **Reduced Risk of Mental Health Disorders:** Good sleep habits and adequate rest can act as a protective factor against conditions such as depression, anxiety disorders, and bipolar disorder.

- **Enhanced Stress Resilience:** Adequate rest can increase people's ability to handle and adapt to challenging situations. Rest plays a vital role in managing and coping with stress. It helps regulate the body's stress response system, reducing the impact of stressors and promoting resilience.
- **Better Emotional Well-being:** Adequate rest can enhance positive emotions, happiness, and life satisfaction while reducing negative emotions such as sadness, anger, and anxiety. It contributes to a more positive and stable emotional state.
- **Optimal Mental Performance:** Adequate rest supports optimal mental performance in various domains, including creativity, problem-solving, and critical thinking. Rested individuals are better equipped to handle complex cognitive tasks, think creatively, and make sound decisions.
- **Mental Health Treatment Enhancement:** Getting adequate rest can enhance the effectiveness of therapeutic interventions.

Myths and Misunderstandings About Rest

Myths and misunderstandings about rest can lead to poor choices that undermine mental health. Among these are:

Myth: When it comes to sleep, quantity is more important than quality.

Reality: Quality of sleep is as important as quantity. It's not just about getting the recommended amount of sleep; it's about getting uninterrupted, deep sleep. Also, there is such a thing as sleeping too much. Sleeping too much can be a sign of and contributor to mental health challenges such as depression.

Myth: You can catch up on lost sleep.

Reality: Although catching up on some lost sleep can help, it won't completely erase sleep debt and can contribute to a disrupted sleep schedule.

Myth: Rest equals laziness.

Reality: Rest is a necessary component of productivity and well-being. Overwork can lead to burnout and reduced productivity.

Myth: Rest is unproductive.

Reality: Rest can increase productivity by improving focus, decision-making, and creativity. And while sleeping, your body is engaged in many essential functions that support your health.

Myth: Rest is solely physical.

Reality: Rest also includes emotional, mental, social, and spiritual aspects. Each is important for overall well-being.

Myth: Older adults need less sleep.

Reality: Although sleep patterns may change as people age, the amount of sleep needed generally remains constant throughout adulthood.

Myth: Alcohol helps you rest.

Reality: Although alcohol may help you fall asleep faster, it often disrupts sleep patterns, leading to poor sleep quality.

Rest Self-Assessment

Answers to the following questions can help you determine if you are benefiting from the various types of rest:

1. Do I feel physically rejuvenated after waking up?
2. How often do I engage in restful activities like sitting quietly or deep breathing?
3. Do I find time to detach from stressful thoughts related to work and other responsibilities?
4. Am I taking regular breaks from screen time?
5. Do I engage in mindfulness or meditation practices?
6. Do I have a safe space or relationship where I can express my feelings openly?
7. Am I overcommitting myself emotionally?
8. Do I set emotional boundaries effectively?
9. do I feel drained or rejuvenated after spending time with others?
10. Am I balancing quality alone time and social engagement?
11. Where I work, live, and play, do I feel a sense of belonging and support?
12. Do I have a spiritual or mindfulness practice that makes me feel connected to something greater than myself?
13. Do I take sufficient time to engage with nature?
14. Am I dedicating time to philosophical or spiritual reading or contemplation?

15. Do I engage in creative activities unrelated to my work?
16. Am I often overwhelmed by sensory aspects of my environment (e.g., lights, noise, etc.)?
17. Do I engage in grounding techniques to offset sensory overload?
18. Do I spend time in environments that are peaceful and calming for me?

Strategies for Being Rested

Here are some practical ways to enhance your ability to rest:

- **Sleep Hygiene:** Establish a consistent sleep schedule, optimize your bedroom for sleep (cool, dark, and quiet), and avoid stimulants like caffeine or electronics close to bedtime.
- **Body Relaxation:** Use progressive muscle relaxation or deep breathing techniques to relax your body when tense.
- **Mindfulness Practices:** Adopt techniques such as deep breathing, meditation, or paying attention to the present moment.
- **Unplug:** Designate specific times of the day when you will be free from digital devices.
- **Set Boundaries:** Learn to say no when needed so you don't overextend yourself.
- **Self-Compassion:** Treat yourself with the same kindness and understanding as you would a good friend, particularly in times of failure or when you make mistakes.

- **Quality Time:** Spend time with people who nourish your spirit. The goal is to interact with people who make you feel loved and understood.
- **Alone Time:** Don't underestimate the power of spending time alone to recharge. Some people find solitude very restorative.
- **Reflection and Contemplation:** Whether it's prayer, meditation, or simply spending some time in reflection, these practices can provide spiritual rest.
- **Nature Walks:** Many people find that spending time in nature has a restorative, almost spiritual quality.
- **Explore Creative Outlets:** Whether painting, writing, dancing, or even solving puzzles, engage in activities that allow your creative juices to flow.
- **Inspirational Experiences:** To foster creative rest, visit a museum, read an enlightening book, or listen to music that moves you.
- **Environmental Adjustments:** If you're sensitive to sensory input, adjust your environment—dim the lights, reduce noise, adjust smells, or declutter your space.
- **Grounding Techniques:** Engage in activities that focus your senses on the present moment. This can be something as simple as feeling the texture of a cloth or listening to calming music.

Books About Rest

Books about rest cover multiple topics, including sleep science, the importance of leisure, and techniques for improving rest. Here are some interesting titles:

The Promise of Sleep: A Pioneer in Sleep Medicine Explores the Vital Connection Between Health, Happiness, and a Good Night's Sleep. William Dement explores the relationship between good sleep and overall well-being.

Do Nothing: How to Break Away from Overworking, Overdoing, and Underliving. Celeste Headlee tackles the culture of busyness and how it impacts our ability to rest and live fulfilling lives.

Sleepyhead: The Neuroscience of a Good Night's Rest. Henry Nicholls delves into the world of sleep disorders, providing insights into how the brain works during sleep and how the environment can aid or hinder restful sleep.

Rest: Why You Get More Done When You Work Less. Alex Soojung-Kim Pang argues that rest is not just a break from work but is essential for creativity, productivity, and achieving more.

The Art of Rest: How to Find Respite in the Modern Age. Claudia Hammond explores what counts as rest in today's busy world and how to achieve it.

Sabbath: Finding Rest, Renewal, and Delight in Our Busy Lives. Wayne Muller offers spiritual insights into the importance of rest and the practice of observing a Sabbath.

Sleep Smarter: 21 Essential Strategies to Sleep Your Way to a Better Body, Better Health, and Bigger Success. Shawn Stevenson discusses practical tips for improving sleep quality and boosting overall health.

The Power of Now: A Guide to Spiritual Enlightenment. Eckhart Tolle's teachings emphasize the restorative power of living in the moment, which can be a form of mental and spiritual rest.

Why We Sleep: Unlocking the Power of Sleep and Dreams. Matthew Walker delves deep into the science of sleep and its importance in overall health and well-being.

Chapter 29

Be Physically Active

"Exercise is therapy."

– KATHRINE SWITZER

"Physical fitness is not only one of the most important keys to a healthy body, it is the basis of dynamic and creative intellectual activity."

– JOHN F. KENNEDY

IF EXERCISE WERE a pill, we would all have a prescription. It is a near-universal remedy as well as preventive medicine. It can add years to our lives and well-being to those years. Getting physically active is great for your mental health.

Physical activity is generally defined as any bodily movement produced by skeletal muscles that requires energy expenditure. Walking is the most common form of physical activity. The range of activities is mind-boggling, and some activities even have the added benefit of strengthening our social connections. Physical activity ranges from low-intensity to high-intensity exercises. The types of activity you choose may depend on your fitness level, health goals, physical limitations, and personal preferences. The trick with physical limitations (such as mobility impairments, chronic pain, neurological disorders, respiratory conditions, developmental disabilities, and cardiovascular conditions) is to find the right mix of activities.

The Benefits of Being Physically Active

Regular physical activity has been linked to several positive outcomes for mental well-being, including:

- **Reduced symptoms of depression:** Engaging in regular physical activity has been shown to alleviate symptoms of depression. Exercise increases the production of endorphins, natural mood-boosting chemicals in the brain. It also stimulates the release of neurotransmitters like serotonin and dopamine, which help regulate mood and emotions.
- **Decreased anxiety and stress:** Physical activity can help reduce symptoms of anxiety and stress. Exercise is a natural stress reliever that lowers stress hormones such as cortisol. It also increases the production of endorphins, creating a sense of calm and relaxation.
- **Enhanced cognitive function:** Regular physical activity has been associated with improved cognitive

function, including better memory, attention, and executive functioning. Exercise promotes increased blood flow to the brain, which nourishes brain cells and enhances their functioning. It also stimulates the release of growth factors that support the growth of new neurons and improved neural connectivity.

- **Improved sleep quality:** Physical activity can positively impact sleep quality, leading to better mental health. Regular exercise helps regulate the sleep-wake cycle and can promote deeper, more restorative sleep. Improved sleep is linked to enhanced mood, cognitive performance, and overall well-being.

- **Increased self-esteem and self-efficacy:** Engaging in physical activity and achieving fitness-related goals can boost self-esteem and self-confidence. Regular exercise allows people to experience improvements in physical abilities, body image, and overall fitness. This sense of accomplishment and increased self-worth can positively impact mental health.

- **Social interaction and support:** Participating in physical activities often involves social interaction, whether through team sports, group classes, or exercise communities. These social connections can provide a sense of belonging, support, and positive social interactions, which are important for mental well-being.

- **Enhanced energy:** Although it may be counterintuitive, because physical activity uses energy, working our bodies can increase our mood, outlook, and overall energy levels.

Myths and Misunderstandings about Physical Activity

Be aware of the following myths or misunderstandings about the relationship between physical activity and mental health:

Myth: Only intense exercise provides mental health benefits.

Reality: Any level of physical activity can positively affect mental health. Although vigorous exercise has been extensively studied, moderate-intensity activities like walking or gardening can also improve mental well-being.

Myth: Only structured exercise provides mental health benefits.

Reality: Structured exercise, such as going to the gym or attending fitness classes, is not the only way to experience mental health benefits. Daily activities like gardening, dancing, playing sports, or even household chores can improve mental well-being.

Myth: You must exercise for long durations to see mental health benefits.

Reality: Research suggests that even short bouts of exercise can yield mental health benefits. Engaging in physical activity for as little as 10-15 minutes can positively impact mood and reduce anxiety. Accumulating activity throughout the day can be just as effective as a continuous, more extended session.

Myth: Exercising more is always better for mental health.

Reality: Although regular physical activity is generally beneficial, overexercising or engaging in excessive training can negatively affect mental health. It's important to balance and listen to your body's needs to prevent burnout or injuries.

Myth: The mental health benefits of physical activity are immediate and short-lived.

Reality: While immediate mood improvements, such as a "runner's high," can be experienced after a single exercise session, physical activity's long-term mental health benefits are more substantial. Regular exercise over time has been associated with sustained improvements in mental well-being and a reduced risk of mental health disorders.

Myth: Physical activity is ineffective for older adults or people with disabilities.

Reality: Physical activity can benefit people of all ages and abilities. Research has demonstrated positive effects on mental health in older adults and individuals with disabilities. Various adapted exercise programs and activities are available to accommodate different needs and abilities.

Physical Activity Self-Assessment

The following questions help you determine your level of physical activity:

- **How often do you engage in structured exercise or planned physical activities?** This question assesses the frequency of intentional exercise sessions, such as attending fitness classes or following a workout routine.

- **How many days a week do you engage in moderate to vigorous physical activities that elevate your heart rate and make you breathe harder?** This question helps gauge the frequency of activities that challenge your cardiovascular system, such as brisk walking, running, cycling, or participating in sports.

- **On average, how long do your exercise or physical activity sessions last?** This question assesses the duration of your physical activity sessions, including warm-up and cool-down periods. It helps determine if you meet the recommended guidelines of at least 150 minutes of moderate-intensity activity or 75 minutes of vigorous-intensity activity per week.

- **What types of physical activities do you regularly participate in?** This question aims to identify the specific activities you engage in, such as walking, swimming, weightlifting, dancing, or playing a sport. It provides insights into the variety and range of your physical activities. Try to get a mix of strengthening, cardiovascular activities, and stretching.

- **How would you describe the intensity level of your typical exercise or physical activities?** This question addresses the intensity of your activities, ranging from light to moderate to vigorous. It helps determine if you are engaging in activities that challenge your fitness level and elevate your heart rate.

- **How do you incorporate physical activity into your daily routines?** This question explores how physical activity is integrated into everyday life, such as taking the stairs instead of the elevator, walking or cycling for transportation, or engaging in active hobbies or household chores.

- **How would you rate your overall physical fitness level?** This question provides a subjective assessment of your perceived fitness level. Although self-perceptions may not always align with objective fitness measures, they can offer insights into your physical activity levels.

Improving Your Physical Activity

Improving your level of physical activity doesn't have to be complicated. Here are some recommendations for gradually incorporating more physical activity into your life:

Start Slowly

- Consult a Healthcare Provider: A check-up before starting a new fitness regimen is wise, especially if you have existing health conditions.
- Set Realistic Goals: Aim for achievable targets to keep you motivated.
- Begin with Low-Intensity Activities: If you're new to exercise, start with activities like walking or swimming.

Create a Routine

- Schedule Exercise: Put it on your calendar like any other appointment.
- Consistency is Key: Stick to your schedule but be flexible enough to switch things up.

- Duration and Frequency: Aim for at least 150 minutes of moderate-intensity aerobic activity or 75 minutes of vigorous-intensity aerobic activity a week, along with muscle-strengthening activities two or more days a week, per the World Health Organization (WHO) guidelines.

Mix It Up

- Include Variety: Use a mix of aerobic exercises, strength training, and flexibility exercises.
- Find Activities You Enjoy: You're likelier to stick to exercises that you find fun or engaging.
- Involve Friends and Family: Make physical activity a social experience.

Consider Using Technology

- Activity Trackers: Devices like Fitbits can monitor your activity levels and offer reminders to move.
- Fitness Apps: Many apps offer workout routines and tracking capabilities.
- Online Communities: Use social media or specialized websites to find like-minded individuals for motivation and advice.

Make It a Lifestyle

- Incorporate Movement into Daily Life: Take the stairs, walk during phone calls, or do a quick workout during TV commercial breaks.

- Stay Motivated: Track your progress, set new goals, and reward yourself for achievements.
- Listen to Your Body: Know when to push yourself and when to rest.

Books About Mental Health and Exercise

Here are books about the relationship between exercise and mental health. They cover a range of perspectives, from academic and evidence-based to anecdotal and experiential.

Running Is My Therapy: Relieve Stress and Anxiety, Fight Depression, Ditch Bad Habits, and Live Happier. Scott Douglas explains how you can use running for mental health benefits.

8 Keys to Mental Health Through Exercise. Christina Hibbert provides actionable steps for using exercise to improve mental health.

Born to Run: A Hidden Tribe, Superathletes, and the Greatest Race the World Has Never Seen. Christopher McDougall offers fascinating insights into the natural human inclination towards running and its benefits on mental well-being.

The Joy of Movement: How Exercise Helps Us Find Happiness, Hope, Connection, and Courage. Kelly McGonigal explores the emotional and psychological benefits of movement.

Exercise for Mood and Anxiety: Strategies for Overcoming Depression and Enhancing Well-Being. Michael Otto and Jasper Smits discuss evidence-based strategies for addressing low mood and stress that is an everyday part of life.

Spark: The Revolutionary New Science of Exercise and the Brain. John Ratey and Eric Hagerman delve into the neuroscience behind how exercise impacts cognitive function and emotional well-being.

Chapter 30

Our Journey Towards Proactive Mental Health

I HOPE THIS book inspired you. There are many great choices for how we can lower our risk of mental health challenges and improve our quality of life. I hope you identified one or more opportunities to incorporate into your unique journey.

As you pursue your proactive mental health goals, consider finding support for your journey. You are much more likely to be successful if you find or create environments that support your well-being. Supportive relationships also increase your chances of success and make it more likely that you will enjoy the process. When in doubt, don't go it alone.

I wrote *We Flourish* for managers and other organizational leaders seeking to support mental health at work. My second book on proactive mental health, *Better Together*, teaches peer support skills, explaining how family, friends, and coworkers can help one another achieve proactive mental health goals. *I Flourish* is a self-help book. It goes into more detail about the 27 proactive mental health behaviors. These three books offer a framework for changing individual behavior and culture.

The current rates of mental health challenges--roughly 50 percent of people will struggle in their lifetime—are alarming. In addition, current approaches to addressing mental health are costly in both human and economic terms. And almost all our efforts are focused on treatment rather than prevention. I see missed opportunities here.

We are just starting to understand the implications of proactive mental health. We can improve our odds for mental well-being. A compressive approach is needed to address all six proactive mental health building blocks. *I Flourish* is a first draft of such an approach.

This book is a work in progress, and I welcome revisions and feedback. What did I miss? Where are the errors in my thinking? Do you have a book or journal article to recommend? Are there groups and organizations that we should acknowledge? Let's collaborate on the next edition. I can be reached at JuddA@healthyculture.com.

Recommended Books

Chapter 1

Allen, J. (2022). *We flourish: A guide to supporting proactive mental health at work.* Human Resources Institute.

Allen J. (2023). *Better together: How to support the proactive mental health of family, friends and coworkers.* Human Resources Institute.

Chapter 3

Hanh, T. N. (2017). *The art of living: peace and freedom in the here and now.* HarperOne.

Kabat-Zinn, J. (2005). *Wherever you go, there you are: Mindfulness meditation in everyday life.* Hyperion.

Kabat-Zinn, J. (2013). *Full catastrophe living: Using the wisdom of your body and mind to face stress, pain, and illness.* Bantam.

Salzberg, S. (2010). *Real happiness: The power of meditation: A 28-day program.* Workman Publishing.

Singer, M. A. (2007). The Untethered Soul: The Journey Beyond Yourself. New Harbinger Publications.

Tolle, E. (2004). *The Power of now: A guide to spiritual enlightenment*. New World Library.

Chapter 4

Aarssen, C. (2017). *Cluttered mess to organized success workbook: Declutter and organize your home and life with over 100 checklists and worksheets*.
Kingston, K. (2016). *Clear your clutter with Feng Shui*. Harmony.
Mellen, A.J. (2010). *Unstuff your life!: Kick the clutter habit and completely organize your life for good*.
Scott, S.J., & Davenport, B. (2016). *Declutter your mind: How to stop worrying, relieve anxiety, and eliminate negative thinking*. Oldtown Publishing LLC.

Chapter 5

Benson, H., & Klipper, M. Z. (2000). *The relaxation response*. William Morrow Paperbacks.
Chatterjee, R. (2018). *The stress solution: 4 steps to a calmer, happier, healthier you*. Penguin.
Greenberg, M. (2017). *The stress-proof brain: Master your emotional response to stress using mindfulness and neuroplasticity*. New Harbinger Publications.
Kabat-Zinn, J. (2013). *Full catastrophe living: Using the wisdom of your body and mind to face stress, pain, and illness*. Bantam.
McGonigal, K. (2016). *The upside of stress: Why stress is good for you, and how to get good at it*. Avery.
Sapolsky, R. M. (2004). *Why Zebras Don't Get Ulcers: An Updated Guide to Stress, Stress-Related Diseases, and Coping*. Holt Paperbacks.

Sood, A. (2016). *The Mayo Clinic Guide to Stress-Free Living*. Da Capo Lifelong Books.

Chapter 6

Chapman, G. (1992). *The 5 love languages: The secret to love that lasts.* Northfield Publishing.

Gottman, J. M. (2001). *The relationship Cure: A 5-step guide to strengthening your marriage,* Family, and Friendships. Crown.

Johnson, S. (2008). *Hold me tight: Seven conversations for a lifetime of love*—Little, Brown Spark.

Johnson, S. (2013). *Love sense: The revolutionary new science of romantic relationships. Little,* Brown and Company.

Levine, A., & Heller, R. (2010). *Attached: The new science of adult attachment and how it can help you find--and keep*—*love.* TarcherPerigee.

Ruiz, D. M. (1999). *The mastery of love: A practical guide to the art of relationship.* Amber-Allen Publishing.

Welwood, J. (1996). *Love and awakening: Discovering the sacred path of intimate relationship.* HarperCollins.

Chapter 7

Horchow, R. & Horchow, S. (2006). *The art of friendship: 70 simple rules for making meaningful connections.* St. Martin's Press.

Hruschka, D. (2010). *Friendship: Development, ecology, and evolution of a relationship.*

Leaver, K. (2019) *The Friendship cure: Reconnecting in the modern world.* Duckworth.

Nelson, S. (2016). *Frientimacy: How to deepen friendships for lifelong health and happiness.* Seal Press.

Zaslow, J. (2010). *The girls from Ames: A story of women and a forty-year friendship.* Gotham Books.

Chapter 8

Casarjian, R. (2010). *Forgiveness: A bold choice for a peaceful heart.* Bantam.

Flanigan, B. (1992). *Forgiving the unforgivable.* New York: Macmillan.

Kornfield, J. (2008). *The art of forgiveness, lovingkindness, and peace.* Bantam.

Lama, D., & Chan, V. (2005). *The wisdom of forgiveness: Intimate conversations and journeys.* Penguin.

Luskin, F., & Luskin, F. (2002). *Forgive for good: A proven prescription for health and happiness.* HarperSanFrancisco.

Simon, S. B., & Simon, S. (2009). *Forgiveness: How to make peace with your past and get on with your life.* Grand Central Publishing.

Tutu, D. & Tutu, M. *(2014). The Book of Forgiving: The Fourfold Path for Healing Ourselves and Our World.* HarperOne.

Chapter 9

Bass, D.B. (2019). *Grateful: The Transformative Power of Giving Thanks.* HarperOne.

Emmons, R. A. (2007). *Thanks!: How the new science of gratitude can make you happier.* Houghton Mifflin Harcourt.

Emmons, R. A. (2016). *The little book of gratitude.* London: Gaia.

Kaplan, J. (2022). *The gratitude diaries: How a year looking on the bright side can transform your life.* Penguin.

Kralik, J. (2010). *365 Thank yous: The year a simple act of daily gratitude changed my life.* Hachette UK.

Robinson, J. (2014). *The Gratitude Jar: A Simple Guide to Creating Miracles.* Wise Ink.

Arrien, A. (2011). *Living in gratitude: A journey that will change your life.* Sounds True.

Chapter 10

Botsman, R. (2017). *Who can you trust?: How technology brought us together and why it might drive us apart.* PublicAffairs.

Covey, S. M., & Merrill, R. R. (2006). *The speed of trust: The one thing that changes everything.* Simon and Schuster.

Fukuyama, F. (1996). *Trust: Human nature and the reconstitution of social order.* Free Press.

Kohn, M. (2008). *Trust: Self-interest and the common good.* Oxford University Press.

Reina, D. S., & Reina, M. L. (2016). *Trust and betrayal in the workplace: Building effective relationships in your organization.* Berrett-Koehler.

Rotenberghis, K. J. *(2018). The Psychology of Trust.* Routledge;

Solomon, R. C., & Flores, F. (2003). *Building trust: In business, politics, relationships, and life.* Oxford University Press.

Chapter 11

Cain, S. (2013). *Quiet: The power of introverts in a world that can't stop talking.* Crown.

Coyle, D. (2018). *The culture code: The secrets of highly successful groups.* Bantam.

Lencioni, P. M. (2016). *The ideal team player: How to recognize and cultivate the three essential virtues.* John Wiley & Sons.

Markova, D., & McArthur, A. (2015). *Collaborative intelligence: Thinking with people who think differently.* Random House.

Sawyer, K. (2017). *Group genius: The creative power of collaboration.* Basic books.

Chapter 12

Cousineau, T. (2018). *The kindness cure: How the science of compassion can heal your heart and your world.* New Harbinger Publications.

Ferrucci, P. (2016). *The Power of Kindness: The Unexpected Benefits of Leading a Compassionate Life.* Penguin.

Hamilton, D. R. (2021). *The five side effects of kindness: This book will make you feel better, be happier & live longer.* Hay House, Inc.

Lovasik, L. G., & Lovasik, L. (1999). *The Hidden power of kindness: A practical handbook for souls who dare to transform the world, one deed at a time.* Sophia Institute Press.

Chapter 13

Brown, B. (2022). *The gifts of imperfection: Let go of who you think you're supposed to be and embrace who you are.* Hazelden Publishing.

Brown, B. (2022). *The gifts of imperfection: Let go of who you think you're supposed to be and embrace who you are.* Simon and Schuster.

Chödrön, P. (2016). *When things fall apart: Heart advice for difficult times.* Shambhala.

David, S. (2017). *Emotional agility: Get unstuck, embrace change, and thrive in work and life.* Avery.

Holiday, R. (2015). *The obstacle is the way: The timeless art of turning trials into triumph.* Generic. Profile Books Ltd.

Chapter 14

Brown, B. (2017). *Rising strong: How the ability to reset transforms the way we live, love, parent, and lead.* Random House Publishing Group.

Duckworth, A. (2016). *Grit: The power of passion and perseverance.* Scribner.

Dweck, C. S. (2007). *Mindset: The new psychology of success.* Random House Publishing Group.

Godin, S. (2007). *The dip: A little book that teaches you when to quit (and when to stick).* Portfolio.

Hardy, D. (2012). *The compound effect.* Vanguard Press.

Holiday, R. (2014). *The obstacle is the way: The timeless art of turning trials into triumph.* Portfolio.

Kleon, A. (2019). *Keep going: 10 ways to stay creative in good times and bad.* Workman Publishing Company.

Pausch, R. (2008). The last lecture. Hyperion.

Peale, N. V. (2003). *The power of positive thinking.* Prentice Hall.

Schwartz, D. J. (1987). *The magic of thinking big.* Fireside.

Wheatley, M. J. (2010). Perseverance. Berrett-Koehler Publishers

Chapter 15

Brown, B. (2015). *Daring greatly: How the courage to be vulnerable transforms the way we live, love, parent, and lead.* Penguin.

Burnett, B., & Evans, D. (2016). *Designing your life: How to build a well-lived, joyful life.* Knopf.

Dweck, C. S. (2006). *Mindset: The new psychology of success.* Random House.

Gilbert, E. (2016). *Big magic: Creative living beyond fear.* Penguin.

Grant, A. (2017). *Originals: How non-conformists move the world.* Penguin.

Kleon, A. (2022). *Steal Like an Artist 10th Anniversary Gift Edition with a New Afterword by the Author: 10 Things Nobody Told You About Being Creative.* Workman Publishing.

Chapter 16

Buckingham, M. (2007). *Go put your strengths to work: 6 powerful steps to achieve outstanding performance.* Simon and Schuster.

Buckingham, M., & Clifton, D. O. (2001). *Now, discover your strengths*. Simon and Schuster.

Niemiec, R. M., & McGrath, R. E. (2019). *The power of character strengths: Appreciate and ignite your positive personality*. Cincinnati, OH: VIA Institute on Character.

Rath, T., & Conchie, B. (2008). *Strengths-based leadership: Great leaders, teams, and why people follow*. Simon and Schuster.

Chapter 17

Burkeman, O. (2013). *The antidote: Happiness for people who can't stand positive thinking*. Farrar, Straus, and Giroux.

Ehrenreich, B. (2010). *Bright-sided: How positive thinking is undermined America*. Picador.

Peale, N. V. (2003). *The power of positive thinking*. Touchstone.

Seligman, M. E. (2006). *Learned optimism: How to change your mind and your life*. Vintage.

Sharot, T. (2012). *The optimism bias: A tour of the irrationally positive brain*. Vintage.

Chapter 18

Frankl, V. E. (1985). *Man's search for meaning*. Simon and Schuster.

Grant, A. (2014). *Give and take: Why helping others drives our success*. Penguin Books.

Keltner, D., Marsh, J., & Smith, J. A. (Eds.). (2010). *The compassionate instinct: The science of human goodness*. WW Norton & Company.

MacAskill, W. (2016). *Doing good better: How effective altruism can help you help others, do work that matters, and make smarter choices about giving back.* Penguin.

Ricard, M. (2015). *Altruism: The power of compassion to change yourself and the world.* Little, Brown and Company.

Smith, C., & Davidson, H. (2014). *The paradox of generosity: Giving we receive, grasping we lose.* Oxford University Press.

Chapter 19

Allen, J. & Ardell, D.B. (2016). *Leading for purpose: How to help your people and your organization benefit from the pursuit of purpose.* Healthyculture.com Human Resources Institute.

Frankl, V. E. (2006). *Man's search for meaning.* Beacon Press.

Sinek, S. (2011). *Start with why: How great leaders inspire everyone to take action.* Portfolio.

Strecher, V. J. (2016). Life on purpose: How living for what matters most changes everything. HarperOne.

Winfrey, O. (2019). *The path made clear: Discovering your life's direction and purpose.* Flatiron Books.

Chapter 20

Brown, B. (2015). *Daring greatly: How the courage to be vulnerable transforms the way we live, love, parent, and lead.* Penguin.

Duckworth, A. (2016). *Grit: The power of passion and perseverance.* Scribner.

Gilbert, E. (2016). *Big magic: Creative living beyond fear.* Riverhead Books.

Godin, S. (2007). *The dip: A little book that teaches you when to quit (and when to stick).* Penguin.

Greene, R. (2013). *Mastery.* Penguin.

Pink, D. H. (2011). *Drive: The surprising truth about what motivates us.* Riverhead Books.

Stulberg, B., & Magness, S. (2019). *The passion paradox: a guide to going all in, finding success, and discovering the benefits of an unbalanced life.* Rodale Books.

Robinson, K., & Aronica, L. (2009). *The element: How finding your passion changes everything.* Penguin.

Sinek, S. (2011). *Start with why: How great leaders inspire everyone to take action.* Penguin.

Sinek, S, Mead, D. & Docker, P. (2017). *Find Your Why: A Practical Guide for Discovering Purpose for You and Your Team.* Portfolio.

Chapter 21

Desmond, M. (2016). *Evicted: Poverty and profit in the American city.* Crown.

Dunn, E., & Norton, M. (2014). *Happy money: The science of happier spending.* Simon and Schuster.

Edin, K., & Shaefer, H. L. (2015). *$2.00 a day: Living on almost nothing in America.* Houghton Mifflin Harcourt.

Ehrenreich, B. (2010). *Nickel and dimed: On (not) getting by in America.* Metropolitan Books.

Fagan, C. (2019). *The financial diet: A total beginner's guide to getting good with money.* Holt Paperbacks.

Klontz, B., & Klontz, T. (2009). *Mind over money: Overcoming the money disorders that threaten our financial health.* Crown Currency.

Mullainathan, S., & Shafir, E. (2014). *Scarcity: Why having too little means so much.* Picador.

Torabi, F. (2015). *When She Makes More: 10 Rules for Breadwinning Women.* Avory.

Chapter 22

Bancroft, L., Silverman, J. G., & Ritchie, D. (2011). *The batterer as parent: Addressing the impact of domestic violence on family dynamics.* Sage publications.

Bancroft, L. (2003). *Why does he do that?: Inside the minds of angry and controlling men.* Berkley Books.

De Becker, Gavin. (2021). *The Gift of Fear: Survival Signals That Protect Us from Violence.* Back Bay Books.

Evans, P. (2010). *The verbally abusive relationship: How to recognize it and how to respond.* Adams Media.

Herman, J. L. (2022). *Trauma and recovery: The aftermath of violence--from domestic abuse to political terror.* Basic Books.

Katz, J. (2006). *Macho Paradox: Why some men hurt women and how all men can help.* Sourcebooks.

Levy, B. (1993). *In love and in danger: A teen's guide to breaking free of abusive relationships.* Seal Press.

Rosenberg, M. (2015). *Nonviolent Communication: A Language of Life.* PuddleDancer Press.

Van der Kolk, B. (2015). *The body keeps the score: brain, mind, and body in the healing of trauma.* Penguin Books.

Chapter 23

Lee, I. F. (2021). *Joyful: The surprising power of ordinary things to create extraordinary happiness.* Little Brown Spark.

Liu, C. (2018). *Sustainable Home: Practical Projects, Tips and Advice for Maintaining a More Eco-friendly Household.* White Lion Publishing.

Selhub, E. M., & Logan, A. C. (2014). *Your brain on nature: The science of nature's influence on your health, happiness, and vitality.* Collins.

Wentz, D., & Wentz, M. W. (2011). *The Healthy Home: Simple Truths to Protect Your Family from Hidden Household Dangers.* Vanguard Press.

Williams, F. (2017). *The nature fix: Why nature makes us happier, healthier, and more creative.* WW Norton & Company.

Chapter 24

Ashton, J. (2021). *The Self-Care Solution: A Year of Becoming Happier, Healthier, and Fitter--One Month at a Time.* William Morrow.

Cohen, E. S. (2010). *The empowered patient: How to get the right diagnosis, buy the cheapest drugs, beat your insurance company, and get the best medical care every time.* Ballantine Books.

Goldberg, S. (2019). *How to Be a Patient: The Essential Guide to Navigating the World of Modern Medicine.* Harper Paperbacks.

Chapter 25

Byrne, P., & Rosen, A. (Eds.). (2014). *Early intervention in psychiatry: EI of nearly everything for better mental health*. John Wiley & Sons.

Hari, J. (2018). *Lost connections: Uncovering the real causes of depression-and the unexpected solutions*. London: Bloomsbury Publishing.

Siegel, D. J., & Bryson, T. P. (2012). *The whole-brain child*. Random House Publishing Group.

Chapter 26

Evelyn, T. & Resch, E. (2003). *Intuitive Eating: A Revolutionary Program That Works*. St. Martin's Griffin.

Graham, T. G., & Ramsey, D. (2012). *The Happiness Diet: A Nutritional Prescription for a Sharp Brain, Balanced Mood, and Lean, Energized Body*. Rodale Books.

Hanh, T. N., & Cheung, L. (2011). *How to Eat*. Parallax Press.

Lugavere, M., & Grewal, P. (2018). *Genius Food: Become Smarter, Happier, and more productive while protecting your brain for life*. Harper Wave.

Miller, A. (2018). *The Anti-Anxiety Diet: A Whole Body Program to Stop Racing Thoughts, Banish Worry and Live Panic-Free*. Ulysses Press.

Mosconi, L. (2019). *Brain food: The surprising science of eating for cognitive power*. Avery

Ramsey, D. (2016). *Eat Complete: The 21 Nutrients That Fuel Brainpower, Boost Weight Loss, and Transform Your Health*. Harper.

Ross, J. (2003). *The Mood Cure: The 4-Step Program to Take Charge of Your Emotions--Today.* Penguin.

Walsh, W. J. (2014). *Nutrient power: Heal your biochemistry and heal your brain.* Skyhorse.

Chapter 27

Fletcher, A. M. (2001). *Sober for good: New solutions for drinking problems: Advice from those who have succeeded.* Houghton, Mifflin and Company.

Hart, C., & Jackson, J. D. (2013). *High price.* New York, NY: HarperCollins.

Mooney, A. J., & Eisenberg, A. (1992). *The recovery book.* Workman Publishing.

Sheff, D. (2013). *Clean: Overcoming addiction and ending America's greatest tragedy.* Houghton Mifflin Harcourt.

Peele, S., & Brodsky, A. (1975). Love and addiction.

Chapter 28

Dement, W. C., & Vaughan, C. (1999). *The promise of sleep: A pioneer in sleep medicine explores the vital connection between health, happiness, and a good night's sleep.* Dell Publishing Co.

Hammond, C. (2018). *The art of rest: how to find respite in the modern age.* The Good Book Company.

Headlee, C. (2020). *Do nothing: How to break away from overworking, overdoing, and underliving.* Harmony.

Muller, W. (2020). *Sabbath: Finding rest, renewal, and delight in our busy lives.* Random House Publishing.

Nicholls, H. (2018). *Sleepyhead: The Neuroscience of a Good Night's Rest.* Basic Books.

Soojung-Kim Pang, A. (2016). *Rest: Why you get more done when you work less*. Basic books.

Stevenson, S. (2016). *Sleep smarter: 21 essential strategies to sleep your way to a better body, better health, and bigger success*. Rodale.

Tolle, E. (2004). *The power of now: A guide to spiritual enlightenment*. New World Library.

Walker, M. (2018). *Why we sleep: Unlocking the power of sleep and dreams*. Scribner.

Chapter 29

Douglas, S. (2019). *Running is my therapy: Relieve stress and anxiety, fight depression, and live happier*. The Experiment.

Hibbert, C. (2016). *8 Keys to Mental Health Through Exercise (8 Keys to Mental Health)*. W.W. Norton & Company.

McDougall, C. (2011). *Born to run: The hidden tribe, the ultra-runners, and the greatest race the world has never seen*. Knopf Doubleday Publishing Group.

McGonigal, K. (2019). *The joy of movement: how exercise helps us find happiness, hope, connection, and courage*. Penguin.

Otto, M. W., & Smits, J. A. (2011). *Exercise for mood and anxiety: Proven strategies for overcoming depression and enhancing well-being*. Oxford University Press.

Ratey, J & Hagerman, E. (2013). *Spark: The Revolutionary New Science of Exercise and the Brain*. Little, Brown Spark

About the Author

Judd Allen earned his Ph.D. in community psychology from New York University. He is president of the Human Resources Institute, LLC, and an editor of the *American Journal of Health Promotion*. His previous books include *Better Together, We Flourish, Wellness Leadership, Culture Change Planner, Bringing Wellness Home, Kitchen Table Talks for Wellness, 103 Challenges for Manager-Led Wellness*, and *Healthy Habits Helpful Friends*. He lives in Burlington, Vermont and Montreal, Canada.